BEN LEXCEN

The Man, the Keel and the Cup

BEN LEXCEN

THE MAN, THE KEEL AND THE CUP

BRUCE STANNARD

faber and faber
LONDON · BOSTON

First published in 1984
by Faber and Faber Limited
3 Queen Square London WC1N 3AU
Set and printed in Great Britain by
Richard Clay (The Chaucer Press) Ltd, Bungay, Suffolk
All rights reserved

British Library Cataloguing in Publication Data

Stannard, Bruce
Ben Lexcen.
1. Lexcen, Ben   2. Yacht designers–
Australia–Biography
I. Title
623.8'1223   VM140.L4

ISBN 0–571–13396–7

For Yvonne

Contents

Acknowledgements

For permission to reproduce the photographs in this book, the author and publishers acknowledge the following with gratitude:

Alan Bond, *The Bulletin*, Roger Garwood, Tim Jeffery, Ben Lexcen, G. L. W. Oppenheim, Quantas Airlines, Australia, Jack Rooklyn, Jim Ryves, Bruce Stannard, Craig Whitworth, Norm Wright, *Yachting World*,

and would like to thank everyone else who helped with picture research.

Ben Lexcen's designs for *Apollo* and *Apollo II* are reproduced with his permission. The charts were drawn by Kevin Barry.

Foreword

After 132 years of competition Australia won the America's Cup in September 1983. For twelve years I worked closely with Alan Bond in an attempt to bring about this historic victory. As a fatalist, I believe that last year's win was the culmination of a series of events which began with our first challenger, *Southern Cross*, in 1974. This led on to the double try with *Australia* and the final success of *Australia II.*

In all these years approximately two hundred people have been directly involved in the long campaign to win the America's Cup. Some have been blessed by the experience, and some destroyed, but no one who has attempted to snatch the cup from the Americans has remained untouched by its influence.

It was a glorious autumn morning in September 1983 when I saw the magnificent trophy as it was presented to Alan Bond and the winning crew of *Australia II*. Gazing at it for the first time, I was overawed. This was the prize that had been coveted by challengers such as Lipton and Sopwith and jealously guarded by defenders like Herreschoff and Vanderbilt. The aura of those legendary figures seems to cling to the prize. As the ceremony wore on, we were encouraged tentatively to touch this almost sacred object, and soon we were treating it with such familiarity that I feel embarrassed to think about it.

Now the Cup is enshrined in Perth, and a new chapter begins – can we now defend the Cup in Australia? For the next three years I shall be working once again to win the America's Cup.

This book is a record of my life as told to, and researched by, Bruce Stannard. He has uncovered events which even I had forgotten. I hope that my humble story, which has been presented in a thorough and professional way, justifies the effort and time that Bruce has taken with this work.

BEN LEXCEN

April 1984

Preface

Long before his summer of triumph in Newport Ben Lexcen was acknowledged as a designer of genius. The New York Yacht Club, of course, pinned other, less flattering tags on him. But to those who know him he is indeed a rare creature of pure creativity. If you believe in reincarnation, as he does, it is possible to see in this bulky, blinking bear of a man all the great natural brilliance of a Nat Herreschoff, all the daring imagination of an Uffa Fox, all the brave, experimental drive of a Manfred Curry.

And yet, for all that, the man who designed the yacht that won the America's Cup remains as genuinely unaffected as if he were flying like a butterfly somewhere above all the plaudits, dreaming his dreams of boats, sails, rigs and speed at sea. Ben Lexcen *is* a dreamer. And in his case that is a precious gift. Ben's vision has not been blinkered by formal education. He is a genuine free spirit, a lateral thinker whose mind grasps the esoterics of nuclear physics or classical music just as readily as it embraces the complexities of hydrodynamics.

He is a leprechaun, a larrikin, a storyteller and a brilliant mime. His life story borders on the incredible. From the harshest of beginnings in a bush tent, through the almost Dickensian rigours of an orphanage, Ben – who was later to say, 'The sea became my parents, more or less' – grew up with an obsession about boats and sailing that was to dominate his life. At various times he has been a metalworker, a turner, a boatbuilder, a sailmaker, a world-class champion skipper and an Olympic helmsman. His broad experience has helped to forge a self-taught designer with a natural 'seat-of-the-pants' understanding of yachts and the sea.

My comparison of Ben Lexcen with the legendary figures of Herreschoff, Fox and Curry – the men who remain his greatest heroes – is entirely fitting. Above all others, they would applaud the design breakthrough that produced the winged victory in the historic America's Cup challenge in the summer of 1983.

Ben Lexcen has an army of friends, many of whom have helped me with their anecdotes and recollections of both the boy and the man. Special thanks go to Carl and Alysoun Ryves, Mr and Mrs Jim Ryves, Craig Whitworth, Warren Jones, Norm Wright, Sir James Hardy, Peter Cole, Alan Payne, Bob Bull, Lou d'Alpuget, Bob Ross, Alan Bond, Ken Berkeley, Dick Hammond, John Longley, Mike Ramsden and Ken Beashel.

B.S.

April 1984

Chapter One

The Boy from the Bush

Ben Lexcen has his own eccentric theory of life. He is convinced that within each of us resides the capacity for genius and that from the moment of our conception we are programmed like computer cards. Circumstances can prevent this card from coming into play but if we meet with the right opportunity then genius will appear. In Ben's view, 'There are probably dozens of young Einsteins and Mozarts walking around the streets of Sydney, London or New York. They are probably short-order chefs or ditch-diggers because they're unaware of their own potential. Their card has not matched up with the right situation. But once it does, *bang*! There's a blinding flash and before you know it there's someone spouting about the theory of relativity or humming a new "Jupiter" Symphony.'

He is speaking from personal experience. Looking back he sees that his own blinding flash occurred in 1943 when he was 7 years old. His family had left the vast, sprawling emptiness of the Australian bush to come to the east coast. He remembers standing on the beach and gazing with amazement at the vast blue Pacific breaking on the shore. He thought that a vast dam must have burst – no one had explained to him that this was the sea. That same day, exploring the beach at Newcastle, he discovered an enormous map pool. The pool, about 50 yards in diameter, was a map of the world, with all the canals, seas and oceans about 4 feet deep. This beautiful geography lesson is now immersed under sand but Ben recalls it vividly. He watched with fascination as crowds of small boys with model boats besieged the concrete continents which were surrounded by the pool's waist-high water. It was the first time that he had seen a boat and he claims that from that moment the computer programme inside him began to function. Forty years later and half a world away Ben would sail a slightly bigger boat, *Australia II*, off Newport, Rhode Island and win the America's Cup.

The winning of the cup from the Americans, who had monopolized this international yachting trophy for over a hundred years, is a sporting achievement that has been compared with the scaling of Everest. For Ben it was the realization of a dream that had begun twenty years before when he first recognized the revolutionary potential of the winged keel. The victory marked a high point in his extraordinary career and it has given him an almost legendary status in his homeland, Australia.

The Ben Lexcen story has many of the characteristics of a classic rags-to-riches fairy tale. It is the story of a self-taught genius and dreamer, who survived a childhood of cruelty and neglect to conquer the international yachting world as a master of design. It begins at the tail-end of the Depression on 19 March 1936, in a tiny sheep, wheat and wool centre north-west of Sydney called Boggabri.

Edward Miller, who soon disappears from Ben's story, is said to have been tall and blond with Germanic good looks. He was 21 years old, a timber cutter working for the state government railways, when his young wife, Doreen, gave birth to their first and only son. The baby, christened Robert Clyde Miller, would later change his name to Ben Lexcen. Shortly after the birth the family returned to the bush camp, deep in the rugged Nandewar Ranges where Miller worked with a small gang of labourers contracted to supply the railways with hardwood sleepers.

Ben remembers his early, nomadic childhood years in the bush with an uncanny clarity. He was kept in a playpen beside a constantly burning camp fire; at night the bushmen would gather round it to tell yarns and carve toys for him. His early memories – of his mother carrying mountain water from the creek, of the blackened billy-can suspended over the fire boiling water ready for tea, the meat-safe hanging from the bough of a tree and the dripping canvas water bag – conjure up the camp-site images familiar to generations of Australian pioneers. Ben can recall the sounds and smells of his childhood too: the crack of steel against wood, the groaning collapse of the giant forest trees, the sharp, tangy smell of granite after rain and the almost overpowering aroma of eucalyptus at midday.

Edward Miller was a restless man and as soon as a site had been cut bare or a contract quota filled the family would move on. In the tradition of the true Australian swagman he spent years tramping the bush tracks from one logging camp to another, from western New South Wales up to the Queensland border. On these journeys Miller carried his son, like his swag, high on his shoulders while Doreen followed leading a reluctant pack-horse. For years Ben's home was merely a semi-permanent shack in the bush fashioned from hessian sacks.

Life in the bush was hard and dangerous, especially for a child. Ben's early ability to survive near-fatal accidents has stayed with him in later life. His mother would regularly have to walk 7 miles to the nearest town, leading a horse with fresh supplies. On one such trip 2-year-old Ben was clinging to the saddle when his mother's scarf blew back and blinded the horse which bolted. Ben was thrown 100 metres down the track but survived uninjured; he has not mounted a horse to this day.

That was just the first of many violent and frightening adventures Ben was to experience. Crossing the swollen Condamine River, with his father one day, Miller fell and the 2-year-old was swept off his shoulders downstream. He was buffeted for a quarter of a mile before landing, unharmed, on a sandbank. When he was 5 he wandered miles away from the camp-site, eventually finding his way home through the bush by following the sound of axes.

Ben's brief acquaintance with his father came to an abrupt end when he was 5 years old. He recalls the two of them visiting bush towns – and pubs in particular – where Miller would sit him up on the bar and stick his pipe in his mouth or rest his huge hat on his tiny head. He remembers his father as the kind of man who would spend his last penny on shouting (buying) for everyone at the bar. Miller's grandiose behaviour took its toll on his family: 'He was the kind of man who would give you his last dollar. Even if he had no money he would make out that he had stacks and he'd run up big debts saying, "Oh, sure, put it on my account." And then we would have to leave town because he couldn't pay the bill.'

Miller was fond of his son. According to Ben, 'He didn't like my mother but he liked me.' The marriage was plagued by violent conflicts. There were vicious, often drunken fights and Ben bitterly remembers seeing his father for the last time when war broke out: 'The bugger went and left me. I guess he left both of us. I was 5. He went off and joined the Air Force. He came home for half an hour. I remember his grey-blue uniform and his piercing blue eyes. He had a fight with my mother and I never saw him again.'

During the war years Ben was slowly abandoned by his mother who left him in the care of numerous different relatives. To begin with mother and son trudged from one bush town to the next, often living in the pubs where Doreen worked as a barmaid. While other children were at school Ben played hide-and seek in empty beer barrels. Doreen Miller, with her dark curly hair, had the striking good looks of a 1940s film star. She had little time for her son: 'The war was on and there were lots of American soldiers around. I was a nuisance to her, so she dumped me with her sisters. I did the rounds of all the aunties, all five of them. When one got sick of me she would dump me on the next. I never knew where I was.'

At the age of 7 Ben was sent to live with his grandparents in an old three-storey terrace house in King Street, Newcastle. This might at last have provided some stability but Ben's grandmother became very ill and once more he was sent to live with an aunt, this time in Sydney. Doreen was working as a barmaid and salesgirl there, 'having a good time'. Meanwhile, Ben was shuttled back and forth between Sydney and Newcastle. His aunt tried sending the unsettled boy to a

Catholic school with disastrous results. 'They kicked me out after I hosed a nun,' Ben recalls. 'I wasn't popular with that auntie any more. After a while I became a bloody embarrassment to the family. My mother didn't want me and she didn't look after me.' Ben was 9 when the war ended and he had never been able to stay at a school for longer than two weeks. His education, like his family life, was practically non-existent.

When Ben's grandmother died and Doreen ran short of relatives to 'dump' her child on, she sent him to a home called Boys Town. It was run by the Catholic Church and in Ben's words was 'a place where delinquent kids were sent by the courts'. To this day his hatred of Boys Town runs very deep. His brief stay at the home was a period of intense unhappiness: 'My mother used to say, "I can't understand you. The brothers are so nice and this place is so cheerful." I told her if she didn't get me out of there, I would kill myself. Every day was like torture. It seemed like a thousand years.' Every night a humiliating ritual took place as the boys were gathered to hear a roll-call of the day's crimes and the punishments to be delivered. 'It was like a scene out of *Nicholas Nickleby*. The kids had to file up on stage and receive their punishment in front of the assembly. Kids received six and sometimes twelve strokes with a strap for trivial things.' Many of the boys had been in the home since birth and to Ben they appeared 'institutionalized'. 'They were little inmates brought up on a diet of whippings and readings from the Bible.'

The repressive, severely disciplined world of the home did little to quell the rebellious Ben. He used to be given the job of cleaning out a big aviary full of parrots. 'They were so mean that instead of giving the birds fresh seed every day I would have to blow the husks off the tops of the old seed tins and sort around amongst what was left.' Sickened by this Ben decided to free the birds, for which he was duly whipped. The boys often had to work in a bakery, making fresh bread which would be sold, while they were left to eat the stale remains. Ben's memories of the home are dominated by its sadistic cruelty. 'I remember they made the kids bend over to be whipped. But instead of going for the backside they hit them on the back of the legs where it really hurt. I remember kids having terrible red and purple welts all over their legs for days.'

It was during his stay at Boys Town that Ben's interest in boats became an obsession which would dominate his life. Someone had given the home hundreds of old yachting magazines and at night Ben would sit over them searching for the magic names of Nathaniel Herreschoff, Uffa Fox and Manfred Curry, the three legendary figures who were to influence so many of his own design ideas. He was a solitary child – 'I was quite happy just being off on my own, dreaming my own dreams' – and capable of amusing himself for hours, sketching on the pad that he took with him wherever he went or listening to classical music. Ben's anger, which is often violent, surfaced in him as a child in almost hysterical outbursts which may well have had their roots in the repressive world of the boys' home. The hosing of the nun and the freeing of the caged birds indicate the beginnings of what was to become the Ben Lexcen trademark – the larrikin prank. Today he admits to being a shy man and he sees his clowning exterior as a defensive trait: 'I get embarrassed in front of people. They see me acting the goat and assume I'm very gregarious, very outgoing. But it's all a bit of a cover-up. It helps overcome the shyness. I just can't sit still with people and I get fidgety, so I clown around. I don't know why I'm like that. It might have something to do with being constantly on the move as a child, never being able to develop any lasting relationships.'

The next move took Ben from Boys Town to Newcastle, where he lived with his grandfather, Mick Taylor, who was by then a widower in his seventies. This silent, shy man, with hands badly injured in the First World War, gave his young grandson everything. Suddenly the old Boer War veteran found himself having to cook, wash and care for a boisterous young boy. Ben remembers him gratefully: 'I was too young to see what he sacrificed for me. But he gave me money, he washed my clothes, he fed me and looked after me when no one else wanted to know. In a sense he became my slave. That's the kind of debt that cannot be repaid.'

Mick Taylor allowed Ben complete freedom. There were no questions asked when Ben slipped out of the old terraced house at night and padded down the dimly lit lanes to the waterfront world of the Hunter River Steamship Company. Under the musty, canvas-covered cargoes stacked on the wharves Ben would dream and draw a seemingly endless procession of imaginary boats. He could even fish through the cracks in the wooden planks, 'like an Eskimo on the ice', hauling spiky leatherjackets up from the blackness. During the great era of sail Newcastle was one of the busiest ports in the world. Hundreds of tall ships came to load the rich black coal that made Newcastle prosperous. Often the sailing ships came, ballasted with heavy iron chains. 'The Chains', a dumping ground at one particular site on the harbour foreshore, became a rusty fantasy land where an imaginative child could conjure himself back in time to picture the heaving quarterdeck of a racing clipper.

Ben, however, was not content merely to dream and he soon turned his mind to creating something more tangible: a 3-foot model of a clipper ship. He haunted the local libraries and devoured Basil Lubbock's classic books on the clippers, the fastest and most beautiful sailing ships the world has ever seen. He spent months patiently carving a lump of balsa wood into an extraordinary model. With great ingenuity he had it properly ballasted with lead and rigged with sails made from his grandfather's sheets. The yards were rigged so that with a tug of a cotton line the little ship could change tacks. Soon Ben was making model yachts, planes and even a model telescope, sending away to England and America for books. A gang of admiring boys sailed the model boats Ben made them, racing fleets of up to a dozen at a time. Watching the effectiveness of his models in the shallows at Marks Point on Lake Macquarie, Ben taught himself the most fundamental lessons in yacht design through trial and error and simple observation.

As he recalls: 'I remember one kid's father was a plumber and he made him a lovely little ketch out of sheet metal. It was nicely buoyant and properly ballasted. It beat all the others hands down. I begged my grandfather to buy me one that would beat it. He gave me a dollar and I bought what turned out to be a real clunker. It was really just a lump of wood with a tin centreboard with a lump of lead stuck on the bottom and a bit of calico for a sail. It had about $\frac{1}{4}$ inch of freeboard and every time the sails got wet it capsized. So I got a chisel and hacked the guts out of it and after it was hollowed out I tacked a piece of wood over the deck to make it light. Then I wrapped a piece of sheet lead around the centreboard. So then and there I had taught myself a few fundamentals about buoyancy and keels.'

Ben has always relied on his own acute powers of observation, backed up by an instinctive understanding of form and shape. Higher mathematics, calculus and the rigours of hydrodynamics were all self-taught, absorbed by a brilliant, undisciplined and often erratic creative mind. As a boy Ben had never seen a real yacht out of the water. He imagined that all yachts were very deep, like the plank-on-edge boats he had spent so much time reading about in old books and magazines. It was through his own initiative that he began to create models with less hull underwater and more keel. When he first saw a yacht out of the water its design was very similar to that of his own models. He was fascinated and would spend hours looking at yachts on the slipways.

'That was all part of my own self-education because I could watch and then relate their performances to the shapes I knew they had under the water. In my mind efficiency meant having small sails go fast. I liked the idea of creating a boat with such a beautiful shape that it needed only a small amount of power to make it go. That's a stupid idea which stayed with me for far too long. The best thing you can put on a sailboat to make it go fast is a lot of bloody sail. That's why all my early boats, including *Southern Cross*, were long, skinny boats with not much rig on them. That was always in my mind from childhood.'

Ben admits to having stolen dinghies from the Newcastle waterfront but strongly denies that he was a 'delinquent'. 'I was 14 before I told a lie', he said, 'and when I did succumb I had the most terrible guilt feelings. I was certainly in a situation where I could have been very bad, but I've always been fairly gentle and I've never wanted to hurt anybody. I've always treated people as I'd like to have them treat me.'

Ben left school at the age of 14. His education had been a brief affair: he began school at 9, spending two years at Bolton Street Primary School and then another two years at the local Newcastle Junior Boys' High School. 'I was too stupid to see the wisdom of staying on,' he says. Many of his contemporaries, eager to have money in their pockets, had found jobs at the local brass foundry. Following his peers Ben began his first job as an apprentice moulder, earning 30 shillings a week. As the youngest apprentice he had to work in the oven making cores and was often badly burned in the furnace which got as hot as 500 °F. In those days the men would simply brush off the molten metal, put water on the burn and carry on working. One of Ben's co-workers warned him of the dangers of the job, pointing out to the 14-year-old that: 'No one here is over 35. They all die on the job. They either get splashed by a big ladle full of molten metal or the dust gets them.' It was not fear, however, but boredom which made Ben leave. As soon as he had grasped the principles of the process he lost interest and decided that he wanted to become a boatbuilder.

He went to every boatyard in Newcastle but no one wanted him. He was not even able to make out a formal application for a shipwright's apprenticeship – this was the first time that he was confronted with the fact that he had no education. Desperate to work near boats and water he even applied for a job in the state shipyard in Newcastle.

Mick Taylor's greatest ambition for the boy was that he should be an electrical fitter, a figure in starched white overalls with pencils and a screwdriver in his breast pocket. 'An electrical fitter was like a Rockefeller figure to my grandfather. He was an old railway man and he used his influence to get me started at the old Zara Street workshops as a storeman's assistant. My job was to check tools out and in again.' In many ways it was a fortunate beginning, teaching him about tools, their uses and their value. The railways refused to give Ben the apprenticeship his grandfather had hoped for but they did allow him to start as an apprentice fitter and turner. It was a trade in which he came to understand the intricacies of metal-working and developed skills which a naval architect with a university degree would never dream of employing. In Newport in 1974, 1977, 1980 and 1983 it was Ben Lexcen the metal-worker who would handcraft the masts and spars drawn by Ben Lexcen, designer.

During the week Ben would travel to work at the railway depot at Cardiff on an ancient steam train but at weekends he could pursue his dreams by going to the Vee Jay Club at Newcastle. He spent hours just sitting at the club, savouring the distinctive smell of varnished hulls and old canvas covers and watching the boats. He was given his first chance to sail when a crew member failed to appear. 'They wouldn't talk to me. They were much too important to talk to a snotty-nosed kid. There was a real odd-bod there who never did any good, and one day his crew didn't turn up, so he said: "Can you sail?" I said: "Are you kidding? Me, sail?" Well I had spent so much time watching other blokes sailing that I figured I could get away with a little white lie and I did. I knew pretty much what to do, but we didn't set the world on fire.' Ben soon graduated from 'sloshing along half-drowned' to picking up better rides on better boats. During the war all the old cedar-hulled skiffs had either been hidden away from the invading Japanese or commandeered by the Australian authorities. Ben recalls the day when skiff racing was revived. 'I remember all of us riding on a great fleet of bicycles, going from one old-timer's house to another, saying, "Come on, get the skiffs out, we're going racing again." It was an amazing sight – all those lovely old cedar boats coming out into the sunshine for the first time in ages.' Ben crewed a leaking skiff called *Adèle* but it was while *Adèle* was out of action and being repaired that he had his first experience of serious sailing in 16-foot skiffs. This was to leave a lasting impression on him, as he watched a top-flight crew, noticing how serious they were about winning and how they sailed.

The boy who up until then had been so steeped in the wisdom of Manfred Curry and Uffa Fox now began to develop theories of his own. At the Lake Macquarie Yacht Club, where his bare feet earned him the nickname 'Paddles', he soon became known as 'the Professor'. He was not content simply to theorize; he tested his ideas in practice, making specially designed fittings for the Vee Jay sailors.

When he was just 15 Ben was given his first real boat – a battered old Vee Ess which he cruised alone all over Lake Macquarie, often sleeping out on the water overnight. This was a practice that very nearly drowned him one night when a violent wind squall came down suddenly almost capsizing the boat. He spent half the night sailing about the lake by himself in the pitch black.

When he was 16 he decided to give the boat away and design and build one for himself, the 23-foot *Comet*. Stubbornly refusing help, he created the vivid canary-yellow and pale green Comet entirely on his own. It was a wonderfully slim, ultra-lightweight, hard-chine racing machine – similar to a Soling and twenty years ahead of its time. In 1954 convention dictated that rudders had to be fixed to the trailing edge of the keel. In a characteristically radical fashion Ben chose a revolutionary spade rudder, positioned way down aft. She was driven by a big main with fourteen battens and a big roach, balanced by a little genoa. She also carried a small, flat, skiff-style spinnaker. The result was an exceptionally fast boat that planed downwind and went to windward faster than anything on the entire lake.

Racing around the buoys – and usually winning – held no particular fascination for Ben. He preferred simply cruising alone, often late into the night, looking at the wind and the water. An Easter regatta on Lake Macquarie brought him into contact with hot Star-class sailors from Sydney. Having bought himself an old, unregistered motorbike, Ben, who had no licence to drive it, began to spend his weekends exploring Sydney Harbour. He had read about the exploits of sailmaker Peter Cole, who had designed a 30-square-metre-style boat named *Avenger*, which was cleaning up the Sydney Harbour fleets, and with his typical, straightforward approach Ben simply arrived and introduced himself. Cole, who was to play a

Carl Ryves and Ben Lexcen aboard the catamaran *Oahu* in Sydney, 1959 major sailmaking role in most of Australia's early America's Cup campaigns, encouraged the relationship. He made a jib for *Comet* in exchange for Monel Clivis pins, handmade by Ben as a 'foreign order' in the railway workshops. On one of his trips Ben was introduced to Ted Kaufman, with whom he began an often stormy friendship. Ben sailed with success as Kaufman's for'ard hand but the two had bitter disagreements. Years later they would find themselves arguing fiercely over who had designed the magnificent *Mercedes III*, the boat that swept all before her in the Admiral's Cup in 1967.

As Ben was spending so much of his time in Sydney, he arranged for a transfer from the railway workshops in Newcastle to the workshops at Chullora in Sydney's western suburbs. His apprenticeship behind him, Ben lived in various boarding houses on the waterfront, never staying in one job for very long. He worked briefly as a maintenance fitter at an aviation factory and then as a toolmaker, but at 21 he took another significant step towards the America's Cup when he decided to become an apprentice sailmaker in Peter Cole's tiny loft in the inner-Sydney suburb of Balmain. The art of sailmaking was about to undergo a revolutionary change with the appearance of new synthetics like Terylene and Dacron, which would replace sailcloth of cotton duck. During his apprenticeship Ben learned the old skills as almost all the work involved painstaking hand craftsmanship. The techniques that he mastered had changed very little since the days of clipper ships.

Ben had discovered a true friend in Sydney, Carl Ryves, the 17-year-old Star sailor who later became an Australian champion and an Olympic Flying Dutchman representative. Like Huckleberry Finn and Tom Sawyer they would load up

Carl's Flying Dutchman with camping gear and sail across Pittwater, just north of Sydney, to camp in the bush at The Basin. There they moored the boat off the beach and rigged up a tent between the trees. Neither of them was very good at domestic chores and after a couple of days they were usually so sick of eating breakfast cereal for every meal that they found themselves cadging meals like hungry bears at a forest picnic site.

The two had a fascination for everything Hawaiian and it was not surprising that Ben then decided to design and build a Hawaiian-style catamaran. *Oahu* was a 25-footer, thrown together in two weeks from scrap timber. Carl recalls Ben being so consumed with impatience to finish building it, in the Ryves' back garden, that he would lash out and kick the hull when things went wrong. On one occasion he got so angry that he tried to set fire to it. So impatient were Ben and Carl that they launched the boat without rudders. Ben sat down aft and steered with a sweep oar. *Oahu* capsized on her first outing having sailed all of 100 yards. Despite such an inauspicious beginning *Oahu*, 'just two skinny hulls and a deck', went like a rocket. Ben and Carl spent much of their time racing the Manly ferries up and down the 7-mile run between the city and the Heads, the entrance to Sydney Harbour.

Carl Ryves offered Ben not only his friendship but also a surrogate family. The pattern of constant moving on and temporary adoption which formed the basis of

'Dicko' Cup winners Ben Lexcen and Carl Ryves aboard the Flying Dutchman *Sidewinder* at the Basin, Pittwater

Ben's childhood created in him a search and a hunger for the family he had never had. No one is quite sure how it happened but the Ryves family adopted Ben – or perhaps it was Ben who adopted them. 'For a long time they were my alternative family, the family I never had. My childhood was a constant process of searching, of seeking out the love I never got from my father. I'd go from one family to another and sort of adopt them, sometimes without their even knowing it. If I felt they let me down as a family then I'd move on and attach myself to someone else.' Mrs Ryves remembers coming downstairs in the family home in Hunter's Hill to make breakfast and finding Ben sound asleep on the sofa. 'The house was always open,' she said, 'so Ben just walked in and out whenever he felt like it. It got so that he was at home all the time, so we put a camp stretcher into the toolshed at the bottom of the garden – it had a wooden floor and was properly ventilated – and he slept there. The mosquitoes were a foot long down there, so he rigged up a mozzie net and seemed to be perfectly happy.'

At 21 Ben was a character of extraordinary eccentricity and an avid writer of comic letters to his friends. He had only one pair of trousers which, according to

Ben Lexcen with Mary Ryves at Alexander St Wharf, Hunter's Hill, Sydney, 1958

Carl, he would wash by standing under the shower and walking about in them until they were dry. Sartorial elegance has never been one of his preoccupations. One particular trick the Ryves family had to endure was his penchant for playing the harmonica under the shower. He particularly liked the acoustics in their tiled bathroom, and he still plays the instrument by ear with all the verve and skill of a professional.

Ben's first sails were made for Carl's Flying Dutchman, *Sidewinder*. No Sydney sailmaker would sell them the newfangled Terylene cloth, but their persistence finally obtained them a bolt of faulty cloth with one edge woven tight and the other loose. They only discovered this when the cloth had been rolled out on the Ryves family's lounge floor. With typical ingenuity Ben cut the cloth roughly to the size of the panels and then cut the irregular edges off with a soldering iron, making himself a straight edge to work from. The sails were so good that *Sidewinder* had no trouble beating the powerful big sail carrying 18-footers on the first leg of their own nor'-east course on Sydney Harbour from Clark Island to Sow and Pigs Reef.

It was then that Ben realized that the future for the 18-footers lay with the pure planing speed of super-lightweight hulls. This revolutionary idea later determined the radical shapes of *Venom* and *Taipan*, the two Lexcen 18-footers which helped to change the entire shape of open-boat sailing in Australia.

Chapter Two

The Radial-Cut King of Brisbane:

Sailmaking, Racing, Designing

No one played a more significant role in Ben's early development as a designer than Norm Wright, the legendary 'King of the Brisbane River'. A barrel-chested, bald-headed bear of a man, Wright built and raced 18-footers with great success. The tough but gentle master boatbuilder had been a crack 18-footer skipper in Brisbane since 1936. He first met Ben in the pre-Olympic year of 1958 when he was in Sydney to take part in the Olympic trials in the magnificent German-built Flying Dutchman *A. S. Huybers*. The 21-year-old Ben, who was then making sails with Peter Cole, talked at length with Wright about boats and sails. Wright's first impression was of 'a painfully keen, bright, unorthodox and scruffy young fellow', and he remembers Ben turning up at the Royal Sydney Yacht Squadron with his sketchpad at the ready to draw the idea that he was trying to explain. When Ben asked Wright about sailmaking prospects in Brisbane he was immediately offered financial backing and the use of a loft in a converted shed at Wright's boatyard in Quay Street, Bulimba.

A month later Wright received a telephone call from Ben – he was at Brisbane Station, asking for directions to the house. Discovering that Ben was penniless, having spent his last tuppence on the phone call, Wright immediately drove to the station where he found a lone figure holding all his wordly possessions in a small sail bag. When Ben arrived at Norm's home Mrs Wright packed him off to shower and shave, thoughtfully providing him with a change of clothing. Norm became Ben's surrogate father and mentor, treating him as a second son. Ben settled in with the Wright family just as unselfconsciously and completely as he had done with the Ryves in Sydney, starting work immediately on making sails for *A. S. Huybers.*

Despite Norm's help and support Ben soon discovered that the streets of Brisbane were not paved with gold. His sail loft was an old tin shed that heated up like an oven in the blazing Queensland sun. He laid the loft floor himself and often worked through the night to make sails for every one of the burgeoning dinghy classes that raced on the Brisbane River. None the less Wright remembers Ben's knack with customers. His workload increased rapidly because of his willingness to spend time talking to people about their problems and his ability to convince them that he could solve their difficulties. His business, Flo-Rite Sails, was soon flourishing.

From the very beginning he was a fearless innovator, manufacturing the first radial-cut headsails. He made an ultra-lightweight radial-cut genoa from grey and pale blue nylon raincoat material for Normie Wright's Flying Dutchman, the entire sail weighing only half as much as a normal sail. It proved superbly efficient in very light air and it was not long before Ben became known as the 'radial-cut king of Brisbane'.

Lexcen's keen powers of observation and his apparently tireless ability to listen and absorb other people's experience are central to his methods and success. He firmly believes that 'No designer or sailmaker can exist in a vacuum. There has to be a constant cross-fertilization of ideas. That's what knowledge is all about. I've always learned from other people's experiences.'

One of his earliest and most fundamental breakthroughs in sail designing developed from a story that one of his Flying Dutchman customers told him. The boom had broken but instead of withdrawing from the race he sheeted hard on and found, much to his astonishment, that he was sailing both much faster and higher. He came to Ben's Brisbane loft desperately keen for the young sailmaker to make him a hinged boom so that he could simulate the broken spar while still keeping the boat under control. Ben quickly realized that his mainsail was too full. 'In those days we used to build them with great big shelves along the boom, very full and rounded down low. Now we know that that is totally wrong, that mainsails ought to be fairly flat low down. That was knowledge gained through practical observation.'

Ben has never stopped experimenting or learning: 'I never tire of bouncing ideas off people. I respect their experience and knowledge, and they respect mine. Tom Schnackenberg, *Australia II*'s sail coordinator, John Bertrand, her skipper, and I are supposed to know a lot about sailmaking. People imagine we must sit around and bore each other blind talking about nothing but sails but we always discover something new. We discuss really weird ideas, like using laser beams to project holograms of three-dimensional sail shapes up into the sky. That's why I laugh when people say I've never had any education. My whole life has been an education – it's still going on.'

In 1960 Ben was nearly killed when he fell 40 feet from a mast. The halyard suddenly gave way and sent him crashing on to the deck and into the water. The boom saved him by breaking his fall. 'When something like that happens there's no time to, as some people say, "see your life flash before your eyes". The acceleration is very rapid between the moment you realize you're falling and the time you hit the deck. All I remember was a fleeting sense of regret and thinking, why me?' For the next six weeks he lay in Brisbane's Royal Alexandra Hospital with fractured vertebrae, a fractured finger and pelvis and a splintered heel. Despite sedation his restless energy soon rebelled against the enforced idleness of those weeks spent lying flat on his back. When the Wrights visited him each night Ben would have long and often heated discussions with Norm about the traditional and the innovative in yacht design. To keep Ben amused and to occupy his mind Norm brought him in a small drawing board, a set of cedar curves which he had made himself, paper and pencils. In hospital Ben had the time to think more clearly about the theories of Manfred Curry and Uffa Fox and during visiting hours he discussed with Norm his ambition to create a super-light displacement 18-footer. They nicknamed the design 'the snake box' as it was long and narrow-gutted.

When Ben left the hospital he was bedridden and in great pain for many months. Once again it was Norm Wright who encouraged him to go back to the drawing board and design an 18-footer. The result was *Taipan*, a boat as threatening to the traditional world of 18-footer racing as its namesake, the deadly Queensland snake. Built as part of Ben's hospital therapy, this revolutionary machine was to change the face of 18-footer racing. She was 'a classic chine boat with a beautiful disappearing chine, a developed round bow and flared sides'. The opposition that *Taipan* aroused was to give Ben a mild foretaste of the scandal and controversy that would surround the winged keel in the 1983 America's Cup.

The huge and powerful 18-footers had been the backbone of Australian sailing since the colonial days of the 1850s. Few legends in the mythology of Australian sport are more colourful or enduring than those which surround the great sail-carrying open boats. Their status was legendary and in the nineteenth century vast crowds would fill Sydney Harbour to watch the often violent antics of the men who dared to race them. As late as the 1950s pitched battles were still being fought between the unruly crews of the 18-footers. By today's standards they were alarmingly and magnificently over-canvased. When Ben arrived in Brisbane he witnessed the tail-end of what he calls the 'go for broke' era in the old 18s. Nevertheless hostility to any kind of change was strong.

At a time when most of the Australian 18-footers were so heavy that all five crew men were needed to lift them into the water, *Taipan* could easily be lifted by two of its three-man crew. With characteristic impatience and impetuosity Ben was so anxious to see *Taipan* in the water that he sailed the first race with a small

Taipan on the Brisbane River with its crew: Ben, Brian Hamilton and Norm S. Wright Jr

Flying Dutchman main and no spinnaker. *Taipan* was greeted with cries of derision from the old-timers on her maiden voyage and was spectacularly unsuccessful.

When she reappeared with a full-size rig and sails made by Ben, however, the situation was dramatically reversed. Ben just missed the start of the race but eventually ended up so far ahead that he was able to take the spinnaker down and coast home under the main. Norm Wright remembers this as 'The most significant race ever sailed in the 18-footer class. It marked a milestone, a revolution in 18-footer design. Eighteen-footer racing after *Taipan* would never be the same. Just as 12-metre racing after *Australia II* has changed for ever.'

When Ben took *Taipan* to the World Titles in New Zealand in 1960 he claims that he was 'stabbed in the back' by reactionaries who wanted the class to remain unchanged. The boat had been built as little more than an $\frac{1}{8}$-inch plywood shell and to increase the hull strength Ben had added a half-deck. While this had been permitted at home, the Australian officials who went to New Zealand suddenly reversed their earlier ruling and declared that the decking had to be removed. Ben still believes that he was the victim of Sydney officials who resented 'the kid from Brisbane'. He was so incensed at what he took to be blatant discrimination based on inter-state rivalry that he attended the next Class Association meeting posing as a Queensland delegate. He successfully moved a motion that the World Titles should be held annually rather than every third year.

Change in the world of 18-footer racing could be resisted temporarily but not for ever. *Taipan*, together with Ben's next 18-foot boat, *Venom*, which was to win the World Championship in 1962, cleared the way for the super-lightweight flying machines which today are rated as the world's fastest open boats. Ben had started a revolution that is still under way. Norm Wright remembers that even when Ben was designing *Venom*, he was looking for a solution to the problem of the tip-vortex. When Ben designed wings, or more correctly an end plate with the tip of the centreboard on *Venom*, he was experimenting with the principle which would prove so successful in Newport, Rhode Island in 1983. Jellyfish in the Brisbane River thwarted this early attempt when they became caught around the end plate and slowed the boat down. In the end Ben had to remove it. If jellyfish clogged up the little wings or cavitation plates on the rudder blade he could easily reach down and clear them but it was far more difficult to clear the centreboard which had to be inserted up through the bottom of the fin case.

Venom like *Taipan* was built with characteristic Lexcen speed and impatience. Norm Wright describes Ben as 'probably the most impatient bloke I've ever met. He used to get very angry and throw things when something didn't go along fast enough.' Ben's temper, which would overtake him in moments of extreme stress or frustration, produced outbursts of sometimes comic violence directed at himself or inanimate objects. When Wright chided him about this he would go 'walkabout' and return to carry on calmly as if nothing had happened. Wright remembers

Venom proved 'poison' to her rivals. The stemhead genoa and 'radiating seam' can be
seen here

building a special soft-pine target board for Ben who, 'used to draw caricatures of the person he hated that week, and throw spikes at them. He got to use it often and that helped release the tension that always seemed to be in him.' Craig Whitworth saw a display of the Lexcen temper on board *Venom*, in the middle of a World Title race. The boat had been built in such a hurry that screws stuck up out of the floorboards and often ripped into Ben's bare feet. They were sailing along when Whitworth saw Ben let go of the tiller and begin to rip up the floorboards with his bare hands: 'One by one the floorboards were torn up and thrown overboard. We kept racing and left a trail of splintered timber all the way down the course.' Norm Wright scooped them up in his trailing motor boat.

Ben's often stormy relationship with Craig Whitworth began when the young dinghy sailor came to him for a suit of what were then 'newfangled' Terylene sails. The demise of their subsequent business partnership in the early seventies later caused Ben to change his name from Miller to Lexcen. Craig was the level-headed one, while Ben was the enthusiastic ideas man. Young and ambitious, they made a formidable combination. They won their first six races sailing together in *Venom* and when they took the German-built Flying Dutchman *A. S. Huybers* to Sydney in 1960 they won the Australian and Inter-Dominion Flying Dutchman titles, beating the great Swedish skipper, Helmar Petersen, who went on to win a gold medal at the Tokyo Olympics.

Before this victory they worked on *A. S. Huybers* in Brisbane. First they stripped the boat back and then they restored it. Ben made all the fittings himself and had lightweight cotton lines especially plaited in a Brisbane factory. It was the first plaited rope in Australia, today it is used exclusively by every racing yacht in the world.

The pair's reputation grew as they won nearly every race they entered. According to Craig Whitworth they were celebrating a victory at the Royal Sydney Yacht Squadron in 1962 when they decided to leave Brisbane and start up their own sailmaking business. With a bank loan guaranteed by Craig's father the men moved to Sydney. It took them some time to find premises. They ended up paying £12 a week to rent an old dance hall above the hardware and grocery shops in Spit Junction near Sydney's middle harbour. Their first sail was made for Roger Gale, the Finn dinghy *aficionado*.

The sailmaking business is unpredictable but Miller and Whitworth were fortunate in that their arrival in Sydney early in 1962 coincided with a particularly frantic period in the run-up for Australia's first America's Cup challenge. The city's top sailmakers, Joe Pearce and Peter Cole, were both fully committed to Sir Frank Packer's challenge campaign. This meant that they could not pay the usual attention to regular customers. There were plenty of disgruntled yachtsmen around the Sydney waterfront prepared to take their business to the young pair from Brisbane.

Craig Whitworth and Ben after winning the Australian and International Flying Dutchman
Class Championships, Sydney Harbour, January 1962

It took time but with the help of shrewd media contacts they established their business and created the impression that it was one of the biggest in Australia. The team specialized in the dinghy sails that Ben knew best, and Craig, the man with the business sense, looked after the books. By the early 1970s they had moved into their own custom-built factory and in 1971 their turnover was $300,000. Ben, believing their own publicity which gave the impression that the company was worth more, went out and bought himself a Ferrari, on the never-never, which he kept for five years and sold to its present owner. It was the start of his life-long passion for fast cars and Whitworth remembers Ben surprising everyone when he first drove up to the loft in the Ferrari. Ben leapt out of the car without putting on the handbrake and as he cried, 'Well, what do you think?', the beautiful machine, its door still open, began to roll slowly down the driveway, hitting several trees on the way down.

Ben's first drawing table at the original Miller and Whitworth sailing loft at Spit Junction. Craig Whitworth is in the background with a customer, 1962

Ben's determination to design an America's Cup challenger, a dream which would cause him to abandon both his business and his name, dates back to the early 1960s. In 1965 he persuaded a small group of optimists to join him in the little-known Whaler Syndicate with the aim of designing an America's Cup winner. Carl Ryves, Dick Sargeant, Peter O'Donnell, Bob Bull and Jim Hardy each contributed $50. Ben was the group's designer, Whitworth acted as the money man and Jim Hardy, now Sir James Hardy, who sailed Sir Frank Packer's challenger *Gretel II*, acted as the group's skipper. Somehow, and even today none of the group will admit how, they obtained the secret plans for *Columbia*, the crack Sparkman and Stephens cup defender of 1958. No America's Cup challenge syndicate could survive on a handful of $50 shares, so Ben persuaded Jim Hardy to approach the newspaper publisher Rupert Murdoch for campaign funds. The attempt failed. Ben then tried the Australian coal tycoon R. W. Miller, with a similar lack of success. Money may have been low but enthusiasm, thanks to Ben, was never lacking. In 1966 he convinced the syndicate members that although the Admiral's Cup trials were only a month away, there was still time to build a boat to his design. Carl Ryves recalls that: 'It was Ben's sheer enthusiasm that swept us all up and carried us away.' Lexcen managed to persuade them that Australia's first concrete boat could be built in three weeks. The 37-footer had a bulb like a torpedo on the bottom of the keel and a separate rudder. It was a minimum Admiral's Cup rating and was very short-ended with quite a wide stern, an oval rudder and a fin keel. Weeks stretched into months and the boat never saw the Admiral's Cup trials. As the cement dried, enthusiasm began to wane; instead of being $\frac{3}{8}$ inch thick, it turned out to be more like $\frac{3}{4}$ inch thick. When Ryves accidentally smashed a great lump of concrete off the bottom of the hull, the boat was finally abandoned.

In 1967 Ben designed *Mercedes III*, his first ocean racer, in collaboration with Ted Kaufman, with whom he had sailed years before on Sydney Harbour. It was a radical 40-footer built in Sydney by master boatbuilder Cec Quilkey, from thin, cold-moulded, glued and stapled laminations of Oregon. The yacht was strong and light – especially in the ends – with a comparatively shallow body and such a hard turn in the area of her garboards that her lead keel became almost a fin. In his book *Yachting in Australia* Lou d'Alpuget writes that in order to find precisely the right place for the keel, the hull was first weighed, then set fore and aft across a heavy steel beam to establish its point of balance. The keel was finally bolted on with its centre of gravity directly below the centre of balance. The result – a remarkably easy boat in a seaway with none of the hobby-horsing vices of many offshore crafts at that time. *Mercedes III* was a design breakthrough, anticipating by years the work of those overseas naval architects who were subsequently to develop Ben's work. Ben remembers thinking at the time how wrong the conventional blending of rudder and keel looked. 'It seemed to me to be quite ridiculous. I

Mercedes III hoisted aboard the cargo ship *Galway* for shipment to Britain to compete in the Admiral's Cup in 1967

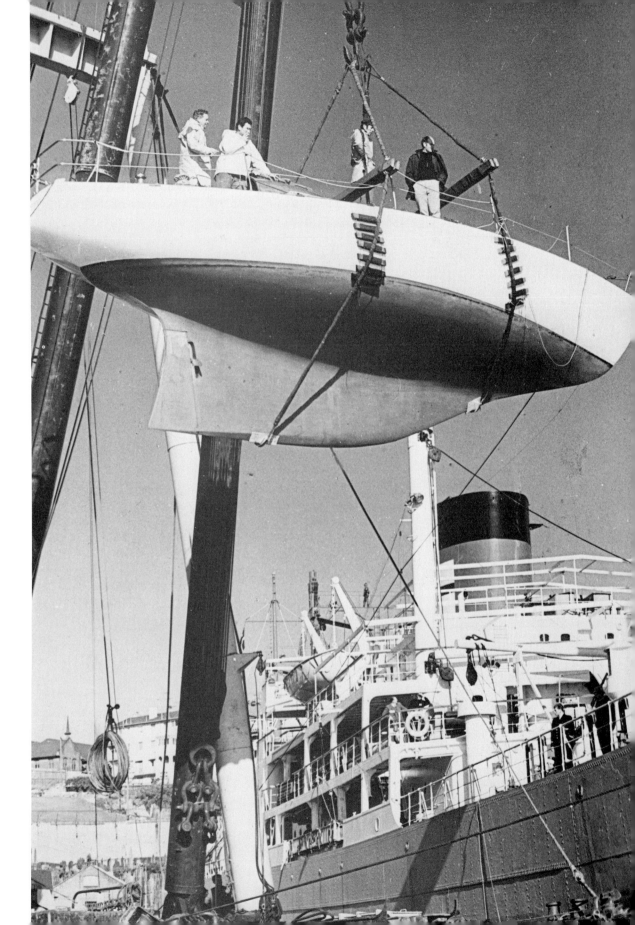

thought, why not have the rudder down the back where you can steer with it instead of stuck on the trailing edge of the keel making the boat roll. It was so obvious to me but I couldn't convince anyone else. No one wanted to take any notice of a young bloke with no credentials. But I was right.'

Mercedes III was a champion from the moment she was launched. She won nine of her first fourteen races and joined the Australian team which won the 1967 Admiral's Cup series with a paralysing total of 495 points, a record-winning margin of 104 ahead of their main rival, Britain. *Mercedes III*'s score, highest of all the cup contenders, made her the world's number one ocean-racing yacht. It was quite a debut for the boy from Boggabri.

In the same year Ben and Whitworth were named Yachtsmen of the Year for their outstanding achievement in winning the State, National and Inter-Dominion Flying Dutchman titles. The continuing success of their sailmaking business benefited from Ben's own phenomenal wins in the newly launched Soling class. The Soling, a 23-foot fiberglass-keel boat, arrived in Sydney in 1967 and for two years Lexcen was the champion of the class. The boats are all uniform in design and sailing them well depends entirely on the skill of the competitor. Such was his reputation, that when he raced *Avanti* on Pittwater just north of Sydney he managed to win despite starting fifteen minutes after the other competitors. 'I

forgot the jib,' Ben remembers, 'so I drove about 30 kilometres to pick it up. By the time I got back on board the boats had already started racing. We stuck the jib on and got to the starting line exactly fifteen minutes after the fleet had got away. We moved down the entire fleet and as we passed the bloke who had been leading he said: "I've been waiting for you all day." They expected me to beat them.'

One of Ben's sailing heroes was the legendary Paul Elvstrom. It was Elvstrom who taught him the importance of 'feel' in sailing. Sailing together in a Soling, Ben watched in astonishment as Elvstrom, one of the strongest sailors ever to get into a boat, reached out and, without the aid of a winch, hauled the backstay on by hand. Awestruck, Ben asked Elvstrom how much backstay he had pulled on and Elvstrom, looking at him as if he were a fool, replied, 'Enough.' 'I said, "Enough? But you didn't even bother to mark where you want it?" Elvstrom replied, "Never mark a boat. If you get it wrong, it's always wrong. Look at the sail and feel the wind. There are no constants in sailing. It's continual adjustment." ' Ben attributes his remarkable success in the Solings to a strict observance of Elvstrom's law of continual adjustment.

When ashore Ben assumes the laconic, almost lazy, appearance of a bushman. Slouching, he sometimes seems half-asleep, but when he is on the water and heading for the start of a race an entirely different personality emerges. 'In the starting area I get a fantastic competitive urge. I become ultra alert and I can see with absolute clarity every little facet of wind and water and sail shape and trim that is going to be important to my winning. I like the feeling of sailing, of having it all come together and working nicely. It's not so much an overwhelming desire to thrash the other blokes but a feeling of desperation or scrabbling and I have to struggle to keep this desperation under control. The more control I have, the better I go.' In the midst of a race Ben tries to divorce his mind from where he is and to ignore his competitors. He goes into a half-dazed, dreamlike trance, concentrating only on the boat. Even when fleet racing, he likes to start without making any conscious decisions but once in front he begins to plan how to stay there. 'I have a few rules which I set myself before the start, like not to tack. Once a race begins there ought to be as few tacks as possible. Even if I have to go behind people, I'd go behind ten rather than tack.'

In 1968 Ben designed the 16-foot *Contender*, which the International Yacht Racing Union (IYRU) chose as its new single-handed dinghy. *Contender* was hailed as 'the greatest one-man sailing machine of all time', and was said to be ten minutes faster around a 6-mile Olympic course than the Finn. Like a miniature Flying Dutchman, she was 16 feet overall with a 4-foot 3-inch beam and a 1-foot 6-inch freeboard forward, 8-inch freeboard aft. She carried a powerful 118 square feet of sail and weighed only 150 lb. In the same year Ben won a place in the Australian Olympic team in Acapulco. He went as a reserve, someone who was

Ben at the helm of the Soling *Avanti* with Jon Mitchell (for'ard hand) and friend, 1969

Contender on display at the Dutch National Boat Show in Amsterdam

expert in all the Olympic classes and could step in as a replacement in case of injury.

Towards the end of 1968 Neville Price, a New Zealand owner, commissioned Ben to design a 58-foot lightweight flyer. It was the success of this boat, *Volante*, in New Zealand racing which led to Ben's relationship with Alan Bond. Bond, then an obscure Western Australian real estate developer, sent a man to Sydney to commission Ben to design a similar boat for his own use on the Swan River. Bond wanted a 58-footer for one reason only – so that he could beat the reigning Royal Perth Yacht Club champion, Rolly Tasker. The result was *Apollo*, one of Ben's most beautiful and most successful ocean racers. Bond had only owned one other boat, the 43-foot sloop *Panamuna*, which he was given in exchange for a piece of land. Once he had tasted the unparalleled thrill of ocean racing in a big, powerful yacht Bond was hooked.

Ben remembers their first meeting in November 1969 when Bond had come to Sydney to inspect the construction progress on *Apollo*. 'I had heard a lot about this multi-millionaire but when he turned up I saw he was just a friendly cherub. He was very humble. At that stage he didn't really know much about boats and he tended to allow other people to take charge while he just signed the cheques. Bondy didn't seem to be old enough to be that rich; I had an idea that all millionaires were old, grey men with big cigars. He gave me the impression of being really rich without being ostentatious. I think we hit it off right from the start. He was always very good to me. He actually let me get on with the design without interfering and that pretty much set a pattern for our relationship that's lasted all these years. He pays me to do my own thing.'

Bond had previously been discouraged by his sailing master and he was forced to take a back seat while everyone else had all the fun. Ben soon changed all that by encouraging him to sail the boat himself. Their relationship is a very close and uncomplicated one. Apart from a mutual respect, the two men genuinely enjoy each other's company. Bond has never made Ben feel like an underling: 'People who work for Bondy work with him. They're not treated like lackeys. He's unreasonable sometimes and he pushes them as hard as sled dogs but they feel like they're working for themselves. He's not a sneaky bugger, he's all up-front. What you see is what you get. If he is brash, well, he's brash. We all know that. But he can also be lovely and nice. He doesn't try to hide the real Alan Bond. It's all floating out front for everybody to see in three dimension. He's definitely not boring.'

Ben has been on the Bond Corporation payroll since 1977 and Warren Jones, executive director of the *Australia II* syndicate, describes the flexibility of that working relationship: 'His [Ben's] arrangement with us is such that he pleases himself what he does, when and how. We simply say we want certain drawings by a particular date but that is the only constraint we impose. Alan Bond knows that he can't demand a nine-to-five existence from a bloke like Ben. He's given him the freedom to dream.'

Bond arrived in Western Australia from London at the age of 6. His father had been advised that he had only twelve months to live and should find a hot, dry

Apollo: the stern profile shows the dinghy-like lines which made her so fast downwind

Apollo clearing the Sydney Heads after the start of the Sydney–Hobart Race in 1969

climate in which to pass his final days – in fact he survived the doctor's deadline. His precociously bright son, Alan, left school at 14 to become a signwriter. Before he had finished his apprenticeship, Bond saw opportunity beckoning in the form of real estate which subsequently made him a multi-millionaire.

Bondy and Ben are roughly the same age and those who know them intimately say that they are very much alike. Warren Jones describes both men as being 'unrestrained by formal education'. 'It may never occur to a man with a formal university education to dare approach some of the weird, way-out things that constantly whirl around in Ben Lexcen's mind. Convention dictates conventional behaviour. Just like Ben, Alan Bond is an incredible visionary. He is the sort of bloke who is not prepared to be bound up by a set of artificial rules. People say, "You can't do that" and he's just as likely to say, "I've already done it." '

Ben describes Bondy as 'an emotional person' and says that this does not always make working with him particularly easy. A combination of Ben's temper and Bond's emotional temperament means that they have, inevitably, had their difficult moments. John Longley, who was crew manager and mast-man on *Australia II* in the 1983 America's Cup, remembers one of Ben's temper tantrums at the time that Bond commissioned *Apollo*. Bond wanted shiny chrome vents on the yacht but Ben had taken a violent dislike to them. 'One day he [Ben] got so mad', says Longley, 'he unscrewed them all and tossed them in the water. They were worth about $100 a piece so Bondy was pretty upset. They had a great wrestling match on the foredeck with Alan trying to stop these things going overboard. Bondy ordered a complete new set but later, during a race, Ben unscrewed them and tucked them inside the spinnaker which was all ready to be set. When the foredeck-hands hauled the kite up, the vents came raining down like confetti. Bondy gave up after that.'

It was during *Apollo*'s preparations for the 1970 Newport–Bermuda Race that Alan Bond first laid eyes on a 12-metre yacht. He had been working with Ben and the crew on *Apollo* at Bob Derektor's yard at City Island, New York when *Valiant*, the radical Sparkman and Stephens 12-metre, which was to be an unsuccessful cup defence candidate, came back from an outing and moored near their boat. *Valiant* was unlike any other 12-metre in that all her winches and all her crew, with the exception of the skipper and navigator, were below deck level. Bond was fascinated and, according to Ben: 'He wasn't content just to look. He was standing on the floating pontoon, peering down into their big, open cockpit.' Vic Romagna, who as secretary of the 1983 America's Cup Committee, would later become a bitter opponent of the winged keel, was down there. 'He snapped Bondy's head off. He said, "How would you like me to come shove my face in your living-room window?" Well that really got Bondy mad. He said something like, "What is that bloody thing anyway?" I explained to him that it was a 12-metre boat, an America's Cup boat, and he asked me, "What's the America's Cup?" I told him

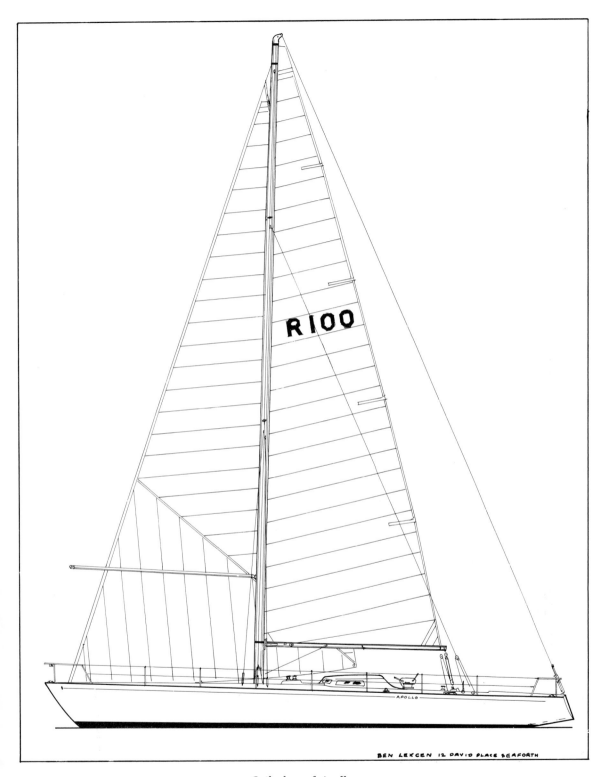

Sail plan of *Apollo*

Deck plan of *Apollo*

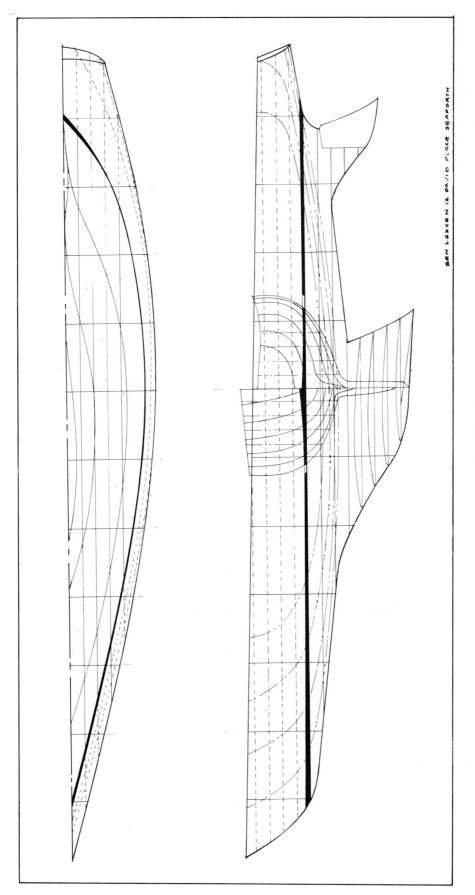

BEN LEXCEN 12 DAVID PLACE SEAFORTH

Lines plan of *Apollo*

and he said, "Right, you design me one of those 12-metres and we'll come back here and win their bloody America's Cup." I didn't think he was serious, but he was. When we got back to Australia he got his sailing master to ring me up to confirm that he was fair dinkum.'

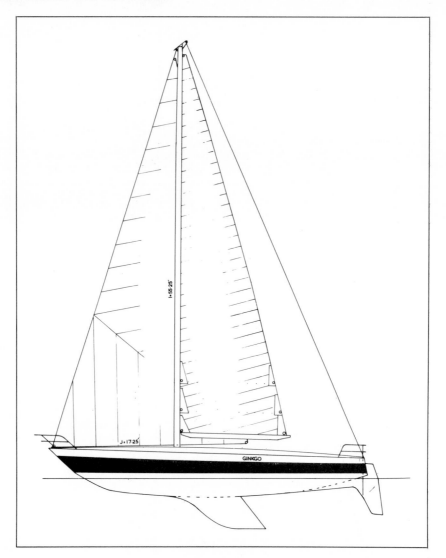

Ginkgo sail plan

After *Apollo* came a string of smaller boats of various classes, all of which were reasonably successful in Australian racing. In 1973 Ben was commissioned by Gary Bogard, a Sydney businessman who had never set foot on a boat, to build

Apollo I in the Sydney–Hobart Race, 1976

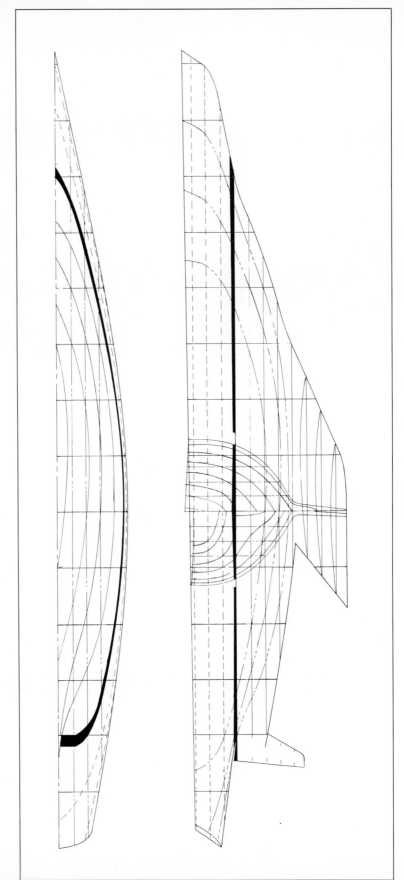

Southern Cross: Lines plan

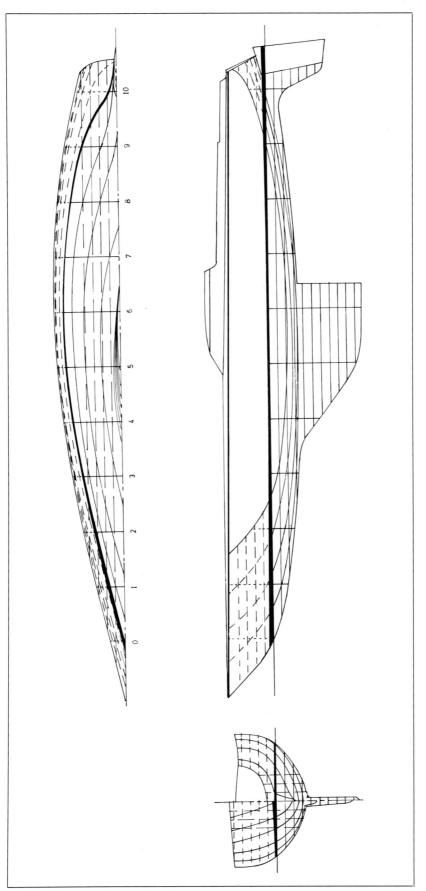

Apollo II: Lines plans × 2

Ginkgo. For Ben *Ginkgo* was a monument to the way in which wooden boats ought to be built, with her spruce diagonal subdecks on spruce deckframes and an interior made entirely from Canadian cedar. She was enormously strong with $1\frac{1}{4}$-inch Oregon planking and Queensland maple 2×1 inch frames every 16 inches. Her shape was the product of Ben's inspired guesswork. 'I had the feeling', he said, 'that fat boats were slow, so I made her really thin with a very pretty canoe body and a terrible keel. It looked like a fighter-plane wing. I didn't even go to maximum draft because someone had told me that you needed shallow draft for racing on the Solent. About all we did that fitted the rules was to keep the stern fairly narrow since I had heard about the penalties you took with sterns.' The Italian industrialist, Georgio Falk, bought *Ginkgo* after her outstanding performance in the 1973 Admiral's Cup series and sailed her with great success on the Mediterranean until she sank after being attacked by whales.

Ginkgo, and *Apollo II* which Alan Bond commissioned, both performed spectacularly in the 1973 Admiral's Cup series. The series was marked by bitter squabbles over a new rating system. Bond had asked for *Apollo* to be built in aluminium to give the Sydney boatbuilders Halvorsen, Mawson and Gowland, practice in the construction techniques which would later be used for the America's Cup challenger, *Southern Cross*.

Chapter Three

The Early America's Cup Campaigns:
1974, 1977, 1980

Money, vast sums of money, count at least as much as sailing skill in the America's Cup. After his disastrous experience with inadequate funds in 1983 Alan Payne, one of Australia's most distinguished naval architects, was moved to declare that the raising of cold, hard cash had become one of the prime essentials for cup competition.

This is not a recent development. Harold S. 'Mike' Vanderbilt, who played a long and active role in the New York Yacht Club's cup defence, once said that if a man had to ask how much the venture cost, he would automatically be a non-starter. The staggering sums involved in building and campaigning the boats has always been part of the special allure of the cup summer. In 1983 the estimated cost was $4 million, and it will be somewhere between $6 million and $10 million for the 1986/7 cup series. The very rich and powerful men who can afford this sport naturally attract other rich and powerful men who enjoy being on the periphery. Alan Bond described this well when he said: 'Successful men come to the America's Cup to be with other successful men. Men who would like to be successful come to be with successful men. That's what makes the world go round.'

Some of Bond's most successful business deals started with powerful contacts made during his four cup challenges in Newport. He clearly loves the way in which the America's Cup places him under the sporting spotlight every three years. The America's Cup may mean very little to the folk in Oshkosh, Wisconsin, but it counts for a great deal with brokers, bankers and the wealthy of New York,

London and Europe. Bond freely admits that the America's Cup has been very good for business.

He attributes his coup in taking control of the Australian oil and gas giant, Santos, directly to his America's Cup involvement in 1980. 'I saw what was happening in the oil and gas industry in the United States,' he said. 'I had met a lot of the leading oil company executives in Newport and when the opportunity came up to buy control of Santos, no one else wanted it. Now I had a great deal to do with the financing of that purchase. It was $37.5 million but I had had enough exposure in previous America's Cup challenges to go direct to the international banking market because Australian banks wouldn't lend to me to buy such a risk investment.' Bond sold out his interests in the Cooper Basin for $190 million and made the largest ever cash profit in Australian business history when he made $66 million cash profit on Bond Corporation's raid on the Australian coal group, White Industries. At the last count Bond Corporation's estimated worth was $A250 million.

It was the extraordinary success of the new Lexcen designs, in particular the world-beaters *Apollo II* and *Ginkgo*, that originally encouraged Alan Bond in his ambitious plans for the America's Cup. Undeterred by the humiliating defeat of the Australian challenger, *Dame Pattie*, in 1967, Ben saw in Bond's enthusiasm the chance to fulfil a dream that had haunted him since childhood. 'When I win the cup,' he said, 'I will be free.'

No one, in over a century of trying, had ever succeeded in winning the America's Cup back from the United States and yet in the early seventies Lexcen and Bond, two Australian upstarts, were convinced that they not only could, but would knock the cup, and the NYYC, off its pedestal. This apparently mad obsession was to dominate the lives of many Australians over the next decade, and despite the knocks and failures of the early campaign for the 1974 and 1977 America's Cup, the Australians' blind determination was finally rewarded in 1983.

In July 1974 the *Sydney Daily Telegraph* ran the headline 'Look Out America' and 'It's In The Bag Say Aussies', quoting Alan Bond's remark: 'We'll annihilate the French and then beat the Americans for the cup.' Bond soon realized that the cup could help him promote his Western Australian real estate interests, including an enormous resort development known as Yanchep Sun City, just north of Perth. From the very beginning of this first campaign a gushing publicity machine, aided and abetted by all manner of gullible Australian journalists, promoted this, the third Australian America's Cup challenger as a world-beater. Such inflammatory arrogance could not help the Lexcen-designed *Southern Cross* (renamed the 'stone banana' by the defenders), which was roundly beaten 4–0 by the magnificent American boat *Courageous*. Designed by Olin Stephens, doyen of American naval architects, *Courageous* was to dominate the America's Cup for the next six years.

Ben now looks back on the *Southern Cross* campaign with a mixture of painful embarrassment and regret, recognizing that it was blighted by the Australian side's misplaced arrogance. He comments that after the success of *Ginkgo* and *Apollo*: 'We thought we were unbeatable. Now that I can look back on it, I feel sick when I see we didn't have a chance against the Americans. Our whole outfit was a shemozzle. It was overmanned and undermanaged. It was just completely wrong. But we learned from it. It was a stepping stone along the road to 1983.'

At the time Australia was in the throes of a financial upheaval called a credit squeeze. Alan Bond had to spend nearly as much time in Australia sorting out financial matters as he did watching the boat race in Newport. While there he was brash and combative in his relations both with the media and the New York Yacht Club. Ben feels that Bond's behaviour was a result of his inexperience and the patronizing attitude of the NYYC (Ben describes them as 'very tough customers') who regarded Bond as: 'A jumped-up little real estate developer from nowhere and they treated him accordingly. I don't think it's at all surprising that he behaved as he did, throwing all those verbal punches at the New York Yacht Club.'

Ben lays the blame for the *Southern Cross* débâcle on his own inexperience and poor management. 'We had the odds stacked against us from the start. We were using a tank which was way too small and people who didn't know what they were doing, including myself.' *Southern Cross* seems to have been doomed from the outset. Ben's design ideas were tested in the pathetically inadequate University of Sydney tank. The tiny tank was intended for student instruction and it was neither sufficiently complex nor exacting for model-testing. Compared with *Courageous*, *Southern Cross* was a very poor second. John Bertrand, later to skipper *Australia II*, had been employed by Ben to develop sailcloth but all his labours made little difference in the face of the US defender's superiority.

John Cuneo (the helmsman) assumed the leadership. Cuneo, an intelligent and brilliant sailor, had never had to command such a complex organization. 'He was one of the world's best sailors at the time,' says Lexcen. 'He won his Olympic gold medal easily and he was a super dinghy sailor, but John Cuneo could not handle twelve people. Cuneo, bless his soul, is a loner.'

Political in-fighting debilitated the side even further, as both John Bertrand, the tactician, and Jim Hardy wanted to be skipper. Hardy eventually succeeded and sailed well. Ben admits that: 'We had a pretty basic sail problem and it would have been a miracle to be the fastest in the world the first time. I went for a long boat with low sail area and that wasn't the right thing. But poor old *Southern Cross*, she wasn't that bad. There were a couple of times when she crossed *Courageous* on the first weather leg, and *Courageous* wasn't even a 12-metre!' He now also sees that for *Courageous* to have been a legal 12-metre, 2 feet should have been cut from her boom. That would have put her down to the sail-area

Southern Cross in trials off Yanchep, Western Australia, 1974

range of *Southern Cross*. But Ben blames himself as much, if not more, than anyone else in 1974 and confesses that: 'I didn't really believe, deep down, that the Americans could be beaten.'

In 1974 Ben married Yvonne Wise, the daughter of an Australian general. When he was 25 he had been married for two years, but it was Yvonne who was to change his life. 'It just goes to prove,' Yvonne says, 'that opposites do attract.' Whereas Ben is a forgetful, dishevelled dreamer, Yvonne is a beautifully groomed, super-efficient planner and organizer. Her considerable business skills have had a steadying, calming influence on the life of the man who still tends to be something of a gypsy rover. With Yvonne Ben inherited a ready-made family. She has two grown-up children and three grandchildren. At last Ben had found the family he had never had as a child. 'Ben is brilliant with the kids,' says Yvonne. 'His greatest joy is to take Adam and Guy, my daughter's boys, windsurfing. It's as if the boys were his own. He's incredibly patient with them and, of course, they think the world of him.'

There are many stories about how and when Lexcen came to change his name. It was during the 1974 America's Cup series that he first publicized the fact that he was no longer to be known as Bob Miller. Ben's version of the story is that he had a friend with access to the *Reader's Digest* computer bank. He asked the friend to find a name that no one else had. Six names were suggested and Ben chose Lexcen, only to discover that there are in fact eight other Lexcens living in America. Yvonne, however, says that after the disintegration of Ben's business partnership with Craig Whitworth, which prompted the search for a new name, it was she who suggested Lexcen. It was a name that came from her mother's side of the family. 'Ben wanted something simple,' she says. 'It took about two days before we decided on Ben Lexcen. There are so many ridiculous stories about the name change but it was just as simple as that. No one calls him Bob Miller any more. He's Ben Lexcen.'

Ben is still 'rankled' that after the success of *Apollo II* and *Ginkgo* he did not receive more offers of work. It was after *Southern Cross*, in the mid 1970s, that Ben produced a series of boats that he would like to forget. These boats included Geoff Lee's *Geronimo*, Syd Fischer's *Ragamuffin II* and Alan Bond's *Apollo III* – all were failures in the trials to select the 1975 Admiral's Cup team.

Ragamuffin II and *Apollo III* looked very similar but Ben had given the Bond boat a noticeable chine in her stern sections which reduced her waterline beam to 11.62 feet. This was supposed to save her 0.9 on her rating of 42 feet. Both boats had slightly knuckled bows, the same easy entrance and the long, straight buttock lines of *Ginkgo*. Narrower, slacker, heavier and deeper than *Ginkgo*, they both had plenty of power in the hard turn of their underbodies which enabled them to carry comfortably a rated sail area of 1,620 square feet. The rudders on both boats hung on conventional-looking skegs, right aft but tucked under their counters. *Ragamuffin II* was 53 feet 9 inches overall, 43 feet on the waterline, 13-foot beam and 8 foot 2 inches draft. She had a total displacement of 35,700 lb, including 20,700 lb of ballast. *Apollo II* was 53 feet 9 inches overall, 42 feet

8 inches on the waterline, with a beam of 14 feet 1 inch and a draft of 8 feet 2 inches. Both boats carried 67-foot masts with high-aspect-ratio rigs with boom ends and mainsheet travellers about 8 feet ahead of the helmsmen.

One of Ben's great ambitions has always been to design a world-beating maxi yacht. His two biggest boats, *Ballyhoo* and *Apollo* (not to be confused with the earlier Alan Bond boats of the same name), were 72-footers designed for Sydney businessman Jack Rooklyn. When she was launched in 1974 the aluminium *Ballyhoo* was the biggest and most powerful ocean-racing yacht in Australia. She was 65 feet on the waterline, with a beam of 15 feet and a draft of 9 feet 9 inches. She rated about 62 feet. Even in 1974 she cost a staggering $300,000. Although Rooklyn, a colourful Sydney yachting personality with a penchant for Havana cigars – foot-long Montecristo Number Ones – spent $20,000 on imported American winches, *Ballyhoo* was far from being a flat-out racing machine. Crew comforts included air-conditioning, essential with the smell of Rooklyn's ever-present cigars, and a huge, all-electric galley. The big masthead sloop had a high-aspect-ratio rig with 160 per cent overlapping genoas.

Launched just prior to the 1974 Sydney–Hobart Race, *Ballyhoo* did exceptionally well to come home a close second in the 600-mile classic behind Huey Long's new 71-foot ketch *Ondine*. Rooklyn had to wait until 1976 before his boat eventually won Hobart Race line honours. In the meantime the big emerald green machine was campaigned with great success around the world, including winning a notable victory over the maxi-boat heavyweights, *Kialoa* and *Windward Passage*. *Ballyhoo* was another of Ben's boats that seemed to be forever undergoing major changes. After coming a disappointing fifth in the Trans-Pacific Race she was fitted with a new keel and a much taller rig.

Apollo was launched late in 1980, but as far as Rooklyn was concerned she was already obsolete. She was a 72-footer in an era of 80- and even 90-footers. *Apollo* did well to finish just seven seconds astern of *Condor of Bermuda* in the 1982 Sydney–Hobart Race. She had broken her boom just thirty minutes out in the 1980 Hobart Race. She was later given a new rudder, a new stern and a taller rig. She was also reballasted several times. The latest modifications, undertaken in March 1984 for the Clipper Cup maxi series in Hawaii, saw both the bow and the stern hacked off so that the overall length of the boat could be bumped up by 1.2 metres.

After the disastrous 1974 series Ben remembers Bond 'who had every reason to be deeply hurt, and may have been, but never showed it, just clapping me on the back and saying, "Don't worry. We'll do it again."' But Ben was inconsolable. Blaming himself for the defeat of *Southern Cross* he decided to leave Australia in order 'to start a new life' in Europe.

He went to live in yachting writer Jack Knight's flat in Cowes. 'I thought that was where the action was. There was very little happening in Australian yachting.

Ballyhoo, San Francisco Cal Cup winner, 1974

The centre of the yachting universe seemed to be Cowes, but once again I know now that I was wrong. The action is where you are. Fame is a very transitory thing; there I was living in Cowes and I just couldn't get a job. No one knew me, no one wanted to know me. The Poms weren't arrogant. They were just inert, there was very little get-up-and-go about them.'

Alan Bond telephoned Ben to ask him to design another boat. 'We had an argument on the phone, and I was really angry so I slammed the receiver down. It takes more than that to put Bondy off; he's determined. He called me back ten times. He kept ringing me and I kept hanging up. We had this long-distance phone fight, he just wouldn't give up.' When Bond did eventually stop ringing,

Ben felt somewhat foolish. He was broke and killing time in Cowes where Sir Max Aitken gave him some work on his boat *Perseverance*.

It was Bond, however, who stepped in and literally bought Ben back to Australia: 'I was in the supermarket in Cowes, spending my last money on a packet of cornflakes, when Bondy walked in all bright and breezy. He said: "You've got no money." I said, "Yes, I have." He said, "You're broke and you're coming home with me."'

Bond did far more than simply take Ben home – he adopted him or at least took him under his wing. By 1977 Ben was eager to design another America's Cup challenger but it was Bond and not Ben who believed they could win. Ben stayed in Australia to work out the details of the challenge before returning to Cowes to work on the design. An extremely important influence at that time was Johan Valentijn who had originally approached Ben in 1973 wanting to work with him on the 12-metre project. Ben remembers dismissing the young 20-year-old as a 'naive kid'. Valentijn had gone to work for the America's Cup defenders, Sparkman and Stephens, and when he met Ben again in Cowes he was able to tell him about their 12-metre programme. His experience in New York meant that in 1977 the Australians were, in design terms, equal or even slightly ahead of the Americans. Ben and Valentijn went to the University of Delft in the Netherlands to test the models of the 12-metre which would be named *Australia*.

After the tank-testing had been completed Lexcen and Valentijn returned to Perth and in builder Steve Ward's yard they lofted the challenger's lines and supervised her construction. *Australia* was a *Courageous*-style boat, but with a stiffer, more stable hull which was about 3,000 lb lighter. By lowering the freeboard and taking a bit of a penalty on length, it was hoped that she would be faster than *Courageous*. Despite a resounding defeat Ben still maintains that *Australia* was faster than *Courageous* but suffered from bad rigging and sails.

Ben was not invited to go to Newport with the sailing crew in 1977. After waiting in Sydney and becoming increasingly frustrated, he sold his Ferrari to pay his fare. On his arrival he discovered that instead of using the mast he had designed, they were using 'the dreadful old stick' from *Southern Cross*. The sails were flat and heavy and Ben found *Australia*'s skipper, Noel Robbins, whom he greatly admires, much more stubborn than John Cuneo. *Australia* had beaten its sister Australian challenger, *Gretel II*, in the challenge elimination series. In Ben's view the total lack of any sailmaking facilities meant that: 'It was a complete disaster. *Australia*'s sails were the worst sails in the world.' *Courageous* won the cup in four straight races and Bond suggested that they should drop *Australia* as the challenger and have a new boat for the 1980 America's Cup. Ben, with characteristic resilience responded: 'Bugger that; there's nothing wrong with that hull. We'll just make a few minor alterations and improve our rig and sails.'

That is exactly what they did and the 1980 America's Cup race proved at last

Ben with Alan Bond (centre) and Johan Valentijn inside the framework of *Australia*, 1977

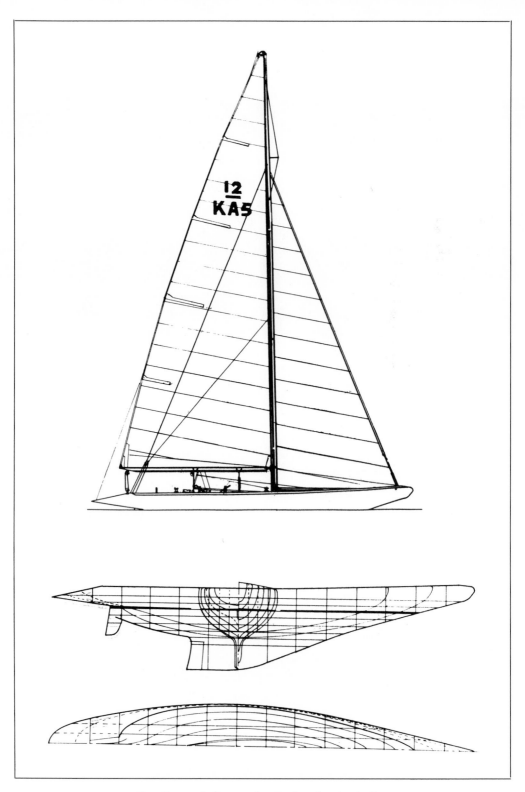

Ben Lexcen's line and sail plan for *Australia*

that Australia could actually win the trophy. The keel on the improved *Australia* was made sharper at the bottom and Ben also lowered the bustle slightly, making it bigger to improve the steering. Tom Schnackenberg, who helped Ben in the sailmaking programme, would also play a central role in the 1983 campaign.

The 1980 match had challengers from Britain, France, Sweden and Australia. The legendary Baron Marcel Bich, in immaculate white linen uniform complete with white yachting cap, was there with a new boat, *France III*. Although they are now on very friendly terms, Bond and Ben had both deeply offended the baron during the 1974 cup. Every time *Southern Cross* had beaten *France* Ben, like a World War Two fighter pilot, had carefully painted squashed frogs on the cockpit to signify Australian kills. The second offence was committed when Bond, irritated by the Baron's interference while *Southern Cross* was practising, turned his speedboat, soaking the elegantly attired Bich. Ben acknowledges Australia's debt to the baron. If he had not introduced the concept of multiple challenges, it is unlikely that they would ever have won the cup. 'We owe the baron a lot. He brought a genuine sense of panache to the cup that had been missing for a long time. When he didn't show up in 1983, he was genuinely missed. Certainly the Australians missed him.'

Ben's fiery temper gets the better of him. He punched his fist through a plywood door in a fit of anger, Newport, Rhode Island, 1980

Newport 1980, *Australia* racing the British America's Cup contender, *Lionheart*. *Lionheart* wears here her extraordinary bendy mast, soon to be duplicated in secret by the Australians

Ben's first impression of the British challenger, *Lionheart*, was that she was 'hopeless'. He was soon forced to revise his opinion, however, when a few days later *Lionheart* appeared sporting an innovative bendy mast which gave the boat a great deal of extra, unmeasured sail area. It was a fortnight later that Ben decided that the Australians should acquire a bendy mast: 'I'd been thinking that the mast was somehow British property and that we couldn't touch it. Then it occurred to me that if we had their mast we could win the bloody cup.'

The Australians immediately started work on a secret copy. They took hundreds of photographs of the English mast: 'the Poms were furious. They tried to push us out of the way. We'd zoom in, click, click, click, then zoom away again. We were like a terribly annoying mosquito buzzing them all day.' When the British mast was measured Ben managed to examine it: 'It was like touching soft, lifeless

A view of *Australia*, the 1980 America's Cup challenger, from the top of her new 100-foot aluminium mast human flesh. They had a rubber sleeve over the fibreglass core. I could see that was the wrong way to go for a start, so we set about making it better.' In the short space of time allowed Ben could not begin to make detailed calculations, so he had to guess. The result was perfect. They made the mast only two doors away from the American challenger in a big old shed without a lock on the door. 'We had forty guys in Newport, but only three or four of us knew we were doing it. We were so scared of it getting out that we kept it secret even from our own men. We had a code: we were going down to the "woolshed" or going to see the "kelpie". We were down there making that mast night and day. Eventually a Newport photographer took some photos through a window but instead of just publishing them he came and told us he had. The guys grabbed his camera and told him that if he published them, they'd get him. I think Warren Jones promised him an exclusive when we were ready to make it public. So he stuck with us and although there were plenty of rumours doing the rounds no one ever found out until we put the damn thing up.'

The fibreglass top varied in thickness from $\frac{1}{8}$ inch at the very top to $\frac{5}{8}$ where it joined the metal. Ben joined it to the $\frac{1}{4}$-inch aluminium section through a long scarf, so that the mast gradually turned from aluminium to fibreglass. This meant

Australia, 1980

that there was no stress concentration, which was important, as they wanted to bend the mast as far as possible down to the jib position.

When Dennis Conner, the American skipper, realized what the Australians had done he was furious. He too had been thinking of making a bendy mast but had been beaten to it. To add insult to injury Ben remembers that, 'When we rigged it up we bent it right back and left it that way under spotlights all night just so that it would annoy the Americans. Dennis [Conner] told his crew that they weren't allowed to look at it.'

After working around the clock to solve problems with the rigging, the hydraulics and cracks which appeared at the top of the mast, the Australians went on to win the third race, and they were 2 miles ahead in the second race when the time limit expired.

The Australians lost the 1980 series only because in Ben's words, 'We weren't man enough. We were like a bunch of nervous kids.' He remembers his own nerves and blames himself for the loss of the last race when he gave Jim Hardy bad tactical advice. Australia made a lot of mistakes at the start of each race and that was enough to secure her downfall, but it was this series which convinced Ben that the Americans were beatable. 'When we won the race in 1980, I knew we could beat them and then when we almost won the next race I was absolutely certain. I saw them panic. One guy ran along the deck and fell down a hatch right alongside us and then they dropped their spinnaker pole in the water. Suddenly their Superman image just fell away and they looked to me like nothing more than panic-stricken kids. If we had beaten them in the first race of the 1983 series, we would have won 4–0. Even Dennis Conner was panicking. They were panicking in 1980. They told me afterwards: "We were terrified." They looked up and saw that bloody big, bendy mast and a bigger mainsail making our boat go twice as fast.'

Making his point, Warren Jones emphasizes to Ben the importance of Australia's winning the Cup, Newport, Rhode Island, 1980

Before the final press conference Alan Bond went to Ben and said, 'We'll do it again. I want you to design the boat, and I want John Bertrand to sail it.' Ben, of course, accepted: 'I would have paid Bondy to do it, because I knew then that we could win the cup. The American Superman myth had been broken. We just needed one little advantage, a technological edge. We had it in the mast. If we had had that two weeks earlier they wouldn't have beaten us.'

Chapter Four

Designing the Winged Keel

The question of how far the winged keel is a Ben Lexcen design is still a contentious one for the Americans. It was Peter Van Oossanen, a Dutchman with a strong Australian accent, who convinced Ben that his design ideas should be tested at the Netherlands Ship Model Basin, a Dutch tank-testing centre in Wageningen, Holland. The New York Yacht Club granted the Australians special permission to work on the design for the 1983 cup challenger at the centre, which is now one of the world's most sophisticated marine research institutes.

The Netherlands Ship Model Basin was started in 1930 as a facility for testing river barges. During the Second World War and the German occupation it became a major centre for the development of German U-boats. Many of these models still hang around the walls. Peter Van Oossanen, one of the principal researchers, grew up near Sydney Harbour. He and Lexcen are old friends. The two men complement each other perfectly, being almost direct opposites. Whereas Ben is the woolly-headed dreamer, the man of inspired creativity, Van Oossanen is a man of pure science, painstaking, methodical and scrupulously accurate. Van Oossanen promised Ben that he could test 24-foot models in the tank. The idea of testing one-third scale models was both new and exciting. At Delft University's tank Ben and Johan Valentijn had been able to test only 8-foot models. The Dutch centre offered Ben the chance to get accurate information from the tank, something which had previously been impossible. By comparison with Ben's earlier test expenses in Australia – the Sydney University tank had cost $1,000 – Van Oossanen's estimate of $400,000 was astronomical. Much to Ben's surprise, Bond and Warren Jones accepted these estimated costs without argument. In March

1981 Ben and Yvonne flew out to Holland, where they would live for the next three months.

He comments: 'I went to Wageningen like a dry sponge. I soaked up an incredible amount of knowledge there. I learned about all sorts of esoteric stuff, like dolphins and what makes them swim fast. It all went into my head and allowed me to see things very clearly and to formulate new ideas. I used their brains, I used their knowledge and their experience. But that is not cheating as the New York Yacht Club claimed. For me, it was like going to university and sucking all that knowledge out of the professors. The process of design is so complex. It's hard to say where one person's ideas start and another's take over.'

After completing his drawings Ben would hand them over to a draughtsman who turned them into specially contracted plans to suit the model makers and their machines. In 1983 this was a point of contention in the eyes of the New York Yacht Club. As Lexcen points out, 'That's just the way things are. You can't go to the tank in Wageningen with your own models. They won't work like that. The ideas come from me but they draw them up to fit their own requirements. You can't be in there like some hairy artist with your putty in one hand and your spoke shave in the other. The facility doesn't allow for people like Nat Herreshoff. Obviously that's the way I'd prefer to work and if I had the luxury of my own tank, I'd be in there just like Captain Nat, whittling away. But the tanks these days have become so scientific, complex and sophisticated that it's just not possible.'

Ben was looking for a breakthrough in keel shape. His first task was to produce a conventional 12-metre yacht, which would be faster than *Australia*. He tested a conventional model with all sorts of different keels and produced a design for a 12-metre boat which was subsequently sold to the Royal Yacht Club of Victoria syndicate and named *Challenge 12*. It was the boat with the fattest keel in Newport during the summer of 1983 and Ben maintains that *Challenge 12* is almost the same as *Australia I*. Only when this boat was completed did Ben decide to use the remaining tank time to test some of the 'weird ideas' that had been in his mind since childhood. *Australia II*, he says, 'evolved from our unconventional programme which was so promising that we abandoned the conventional one'. Ben had not wanted to build *Challenge 12* at all but Alan Bond had insisted, wanting something conventional to fall back on.

Wageningen is totally self-contained. Everything, including the models and all the instruments that monitor them, is made on the spot and can be remade overnight. To Ben it was paradise: 'I used to hang around and watch them tow ships or anything in the tank. It's like a huge heaven for marine people. I've always figured that when I die and go to heaven, this is what it will be like. I'll have lots of time to play with all the models. It was like the map pool in Newcastle, exactly the same sort of fascination.'

Peter Van Oossanen had perfected a method of towing model boats by the mast, an idea originally developed in Canada. This was important to Ben, as it provided an entirely new way of testing: 'The conventional towing point is from the centre of buoyancy within the hull and the boat's heel is set up artificially by a small servo-motor which drives the weight athwartships and tips it. Our models had correct stability. The tow-point is attached some way up the rig which helps induce a bow-down attitude just as the sails depress the bow into the water, and the boat generates its own yaw and heel. The model sets itself up perfectly.' The tank was about 700 feet long and 30 feet wide; the perfect miniature models made from wood with lead keels measured about 23 feet. This was the first time that the centre had ever tested yacht designs and Ben's faith in the staff proved to be well placed. 'I figured, what the hell, they're Dutch. They know water better than anyone else in the world; look at their history. They were the greatest navigators the world has ever seen. They had experience and I figured they would have the commonsense approach that I liked.'

Ben had tried the winged keel idea before and he was unsure whether it would work. 'I had convinced myself that the penalties I would pay in extra wetted surface would be too high. But when we were in Holland with Peter we talked about all sorts of weird ideas and it came up and just grew from there. It became more and more realistic because he showed enthusiasm and put his little bit in. I had tried fins or wings on 5.5s and dinghies and they never worked or if they did I couldn't tell the difference. The upside-down keel was originally invented by Uffa Fox, who put the inverse tapered keel on the Flying Fifteen. John Spencer, the New Zealander who designed the Cherubs, also used this concept in his yacht. Ben 'tossed ideas around' with Peter Van Oossanen and Dr Joop Sloof, an aerodynamicist with the Dutch National Aerospace Laboratory in Amsterdam. He remembers this as an intensely creative period. 'I bounced my ideas off them. They either confirmed them or knocked them down. If they sounded halfway reasonable, then I went away and did the drawings. As for the wings, well we were sitting around discussing all the force we were generating down deep and the fact that the tip would lose x per cent of it. It was a spontaneous realization. Aircraft overcome the same problem with winglets, so we decided to stick winglets on the keel and see what would happen.' They then of course had to calculate the size and shape of the winglets and fed different alternatives into a computer to come up with an optimum.

Ben took about a week to make the model of *Australia II*. There was an intense air of excitement every time they sent the boat down the tank. The first time the model was towed, disaster ensued. The rig collapsed, the chain plates pulled out and the mast fell off. The model careered across the tank, running into and sinking several other models. Ben was dismayed: 'I thought, good God, these guys don't know what they're doing. We had done all the preparation, all this time had gone

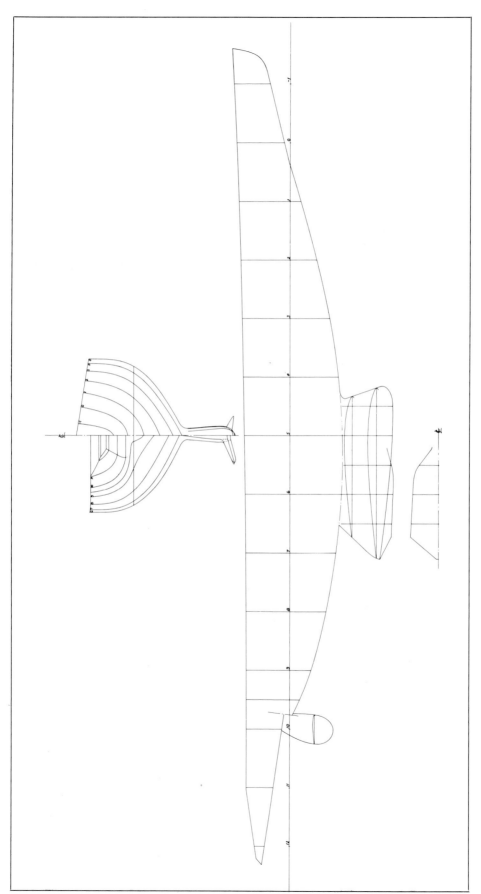

The winged keel

by. I was seriously thinking how I could go somewhere else, where could I go? I didn't know how to tell them that this was not going to work.' Ben's original faith in Peter Van Oossanen did not waver for long. By the following morning the wrecked model had been entirely rebuilt. After the initial catastrophe the *Australia II* model went 'like silk' from then on.

The first keel that they tested was an inverted one without winglets. Ben wanted to make the keel very big because he was worried that a small keel might go sideways. Initially they made the keel too large but the tests did show that they were on the right track. What then developed was the result of trial and error. Ben recalls his thoughts when developing the keel: 'OK, this yacht needed a keel, something to stop it going sideways. It does that in two ways: (a) by its hydro-dynamic efficiency and (b) by having a low centre of gravity which keeps the yacht upright. You put the weight down low. You could put a big lead torpedo on the bottom of the keel but then it becomes a no-lift surface. They're so round, they don't generate any lift. You just finish up with a whole pile of wetted surface. We wanted maximum volume in the least amount of area. Anything that pokes out anywhere is a bad deal for wetted surface. But what if we poked some protrusion out of the sides which was flat and didn't generate lift? Then we had to work out whether the increased lift would be sufficient to cancel the increased wetted surface. The winglets on the Lear jets were the ones that interested us most because they were handling tip losses and increasing the performance of those planes way beyond their size. We realized that the wings were going to be a big penalty in terms of wetted surface but they did have the added attraction of putting a lot of weight down low, so we had to try to make them as small as possible and consist-ent with doing a good job. That's where we used the computer. The wings block the vortex, which is simply water leaking from one side of the keel to the other and moving along so that it spins around. The bottom 2 feet of any keel do not generate any lift because that is wiped out by the water escaping from the high- to low-pressure side. Because our inverted keel had a very big lower edge, we stood to lose a correspondingly large amount of lift. We realized it would stop the lift better if the wings went right to the front of the keel but then the wetted surface would be a killer. We had to discover how short a chord – that's the fore and aft measurement – we could have on those wings. The English challenger, *Victory 83*, went for dinky little ones while we went for 6-foot long wings on our 12-foot keel. We made mathematical models of them, from full chord to 25 per cent chord in 10 per cent increments, and we got a curve. We figured that at 60 per cent of the chord we would get almost the same effect as if it were the full length. We made them as small as we possibly could; the optimum was 60 per cent of the chord.'

When it came to calculating the width of the wings, they had to come up with the lowest possible concentration of weight with the minimum surface area. This

Sail plan of *Australia II*

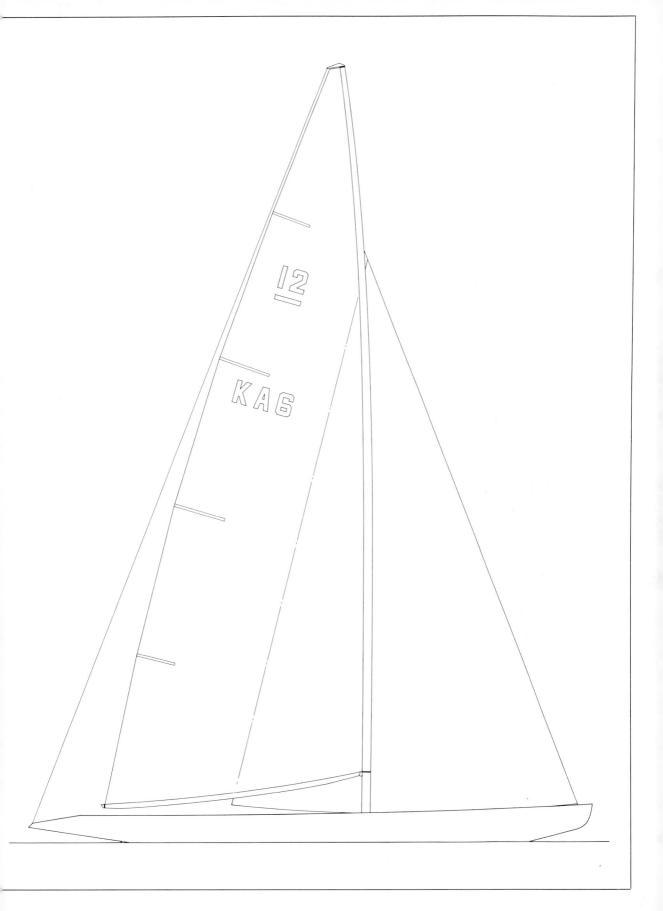

turned out to be a relatively simple geometrical problem. In order to find out at what angles the wing should be Ben originally intended to make several models which would have been extremely expensive. The men at the centre came up with the idea of putting a shaft through the base of the keel and attaching the wings to the shaft so that they could adjust them up and down 2° or 3°. They then put strain gauges on the shaft so that they could measure it bending. After each run in the tank they sent a diver down to adjust the wings up or down $\frac{1}{2}°$ until they found the angle which did not bend the shaft which meant that the winglets were no longer developing any lift.

The net result is that the boat makes less leeway. A normal boat makes about 3° or 4° of leeway, while *Australia II* makes 2° or 3°. In simple terms this means that *Australia II* sails a shorter course. 'If we go a 100 yards forward, we go only 10 yards sideways. Conventional boats are making maybe 20 yards sideways for every 100 yards they gain.'

In the light of the Americans' claims that the winged keel was designed by Lexcen's Dutch colleagues, Ben is adamant that Dr Joop Sloof for one, never did anything that was not discussed with him first. He points out that the reason he went to the tank was to conduct research, 'And research is all about using the tank like a tool not a judge. The Americans expected me to arrive at the tank with my model all neatly finalized. That's what they do. And that's why they haven't been a success.' Joop Sloof worked under instructions; he conducted the tests and came back to Ben with the results. 'I asked him to do all sorts of tests, like putting winglets on the top of the mast and assessing what difference it would make to bring the boom down so low that it would touch the deck.' Dr Sloof would put the details into his computer and when he returned with his calculations Ben would go back to the drawing board. His drawings were then given to the draughtsmen, who redrew them for the model makers.

When Ben was in America during the trials he was doubtful as to whether they had got *Australia II* right. Both the model and the real boat showed a 'funny wave train which used to worry the hell out of me. All my instincts told me it was wrong. And it is wrong. The boat is not good. I know I can make a much faster hull. When we were working on the design we were trying out keel ideas, not boats, and I never let them change the hull. That is why the hull is not very good. The best boat in the world for waves is *Australia I*. It has a perfect quarter wave that goes down and comes up way aft of the boat. *Australia II*'s quarter wave comes up halfway along the boat and then goes down again. The helmsman stands at the peak of the quarter wave. Then it begins to go down. In all the other good boats, ones like *Courageous* and *Gretel II*, the quarter wave comes up aft. That's why *Australia II* doesn't go well on the reaches.'

With his work in Holland nearly complete, Ben's biggest worry was that Alan Bond would reject the winged keel. He had told no one what he had been doing and international telecommunications with Australia had been virtually cut off by a trade union strike. Ben sent telexes home and waited weeks for replies. 'It was like being on another planet, like E.T. trying to phone home. I sent pathetic little messages: "Australia, are you still down there?"' Eventually Bond arrived in Holland with John Bertrand who was to be *Australia II*'s skipper. According to Ben, Bertrand remained extremely sceptical and only began to have confidence in the boat after they had been in Newport for several months. Bond's initial reaction was one of incredulity but after he had asked several questions and had been reassured by Peter Van Oossanen, he took to the idea 'like an excited little boy with a new toy'. They agreed that the keel should be kept a strict secret. But Ben suspects that Bond went straight out and told all his friends. 'I know that happened because Peter Briggs [a Western Australian entrepreneur] went to London and told Peter de Savary. Bondy insisted on complete secrecy and then enthusiastically went out and told fifty people.'

When Ben returned to Sydney and showed his plans to boatbuilder Steve Ward he was greeted with disbelief. It was hardly surprising. As Ben admits: 'It doesn't look smooth or sleek or anything. In fact it looks quite odd. But we grew to like it. When we were measuring it up in that enormous empty shed at Cove Haven, it just sat there balanced on the keel and that was the first time we could stand back and have a really good look at the whole thing. It really looked good. It looked like a giant Plesiosaur with wonderful rounded flippers.'

Chapter Five

The New York Yacht Club and the Winged Keel Controversy

The saga of *Australia II*'s winged keel ranks as one of the most hard-fought and bitter battles in the history of the America's Cup. Beginning in spring 1983 before *Australia II* arrived in Newport, the dispute ran on into September of that year and threatened not only the twenty-fifth challenge but also the very future of the cup competition itself.

In every Australian challenge since 1962 there has been some kind of major dispute with the cup's hosts, the New York Yacht Club. The man behind Australia's original America's Cup challenge, newspaper tycoon Sir Frank Packer, used to say that protesting to the NYYC was like complaining to your mother-in-law about your wife. A sympathetic hearing was out of the question.

The NYYC has received this kind of press criticism since it entertained the very first cup challenge in 1870. A total of 113 years of press hostility towards a single organization might be considered something of a record but the reasons for it have never really been sought by the club itself. It was an antipathy that Alan Bond and Warren Jones were able to exploit very successfully in 1983. The media were only too happy to see the Australians as the underdogs, mercilessly attacked by a pack of brutish oligarchs, the men who, as Ben put it, 'ruled the world'.

Tony Gibbs, writing in the *New Yorker*, has described the stormy relationship between the NYYC and the press as one determined by envy. In his view it is: 'simply envy of the visibly wealthy by the not-wealthy, an envy aggravated when the wealthy do not appear to be persons of much consequence, aside from their wealth, and the not-wealthy are people who consider themselves clever and attractive and whose business it is to suspect wealth.' He also pointed out that the NYYC's representatives are men who are not accustomed to having a gentleman's given word questioned, while the press is – or ought to be – always mindful of Ralph Waldo Emerson's observation: 'The louder he talked of his honour, the faster we counted our spoons.'

For its own part the NYYC is deeply suspicious of outsiders, most notably the press. On 7 September Commodore Robert G. Stone Jr sent an official letter to the members of the club in which he stated: 'There has been a great amount of misinformation and slanted comment in the press, most of it uninformed, and, as always seems to happen, from James Ashbury in 1870 [the first challenger] on through Lord Dunraven and to the present day, the New York Yacht Club has taken a considerable amount of abuse.' He went on to express the club's characteristically defensive view of its own lenient behaviour in administrating the America's Cup:

> The history of the America's Cup has been one of continuous easing of restrictions on the challengers from Commodore John Cox Steven's initial concept that the cup was to be competed for in the way that American won it. This was to sail across the ocean and defeat a fleet of local boats in their own waters. Practically the only restriction left is that a challenger must be designed and built in her home country and sailed by nationals of that country.

A more objective commentator might suggest that it is the nature of the cup competition itself which has changed over the years, forcing the conditions that govern the racing to change also, a process which is usually accomplished only after long and acrimonious negotiations between defender and challenger. The New York Yacht Club's slightly pious view of itself undermines its very considerable efforts in recent years to make the administration of the America's Cup evenhanded. It has done this most effectively by establishing international juries to rule on all matters between competitors. The club's insistence that the rules have always been fair handed undermines the credibility of its good work.

In 1983 the cast of the prestigious America's Cup Committee of the NYYC included former 12-metre sailors Bob McCullough as chairman; Victor Romagna as secretary; Robert Bavier Jr; Briggs Cunningham; Stanley Livingstone Jr; and Emil (Bus) Mosbacher Jr, then Club Vice-Commodore and now Commodore. It was Victor Romagna's outburst back in 1970 that had set Alan Bond on the road to winning the America's Cup. Briggs Cunningham, who had sailed aboard *Columbia*, the first 12-metre to defend the cup in 1958, was an embodiment of the 'old guard' of the NYYC but it was Bus Mosbacher and Bob McCullough, the remote power behind the committee, who were the central protagonists in the keel drama.

Bus Mosbacher, a former White House Chief of Protocol who had defended the cup in 1962 and 1967, is still considered one of America's finest helmsmen.

He is renowned for his toughness. Once during an America's Cup campaign he is said to have told his crew: 'There is no democracy here. However, I do like to hear any well thought out, reasonable suggestion. Once.' Mosbacher was the *only* member of the committee who made any real effort to explain the NYYC's position in Newport when I was covering the cup races for Australian newspapers, radio and television.

America's attempts to uncover the keel's secrets started long before *Australia II* reached Newport. While the boat was still halfway across the Pacific, aboard the British container ship *ACT II*, mast-man John Longley cabled David Wallace, the engineer who had been sent to look after the yacht during its voyage: 'Beware interlopers in US ports.' When Wallace realized what this meant he decided that: 'There was no way we were going to allow any picture-taking. When we came up the Mississippi Canal toward New Orleans I got talking to the American pilot and he told me that the ship's agent would come on board, say he was a yachty and ask for a quick peek. The pilot warned me this bloke's employer had a son who was sailing with the *Freedom–Liberty* mob. Sure enough he tried to look. Every time we came into a US port there were always plenty of well-spoken, well-dressed "longshoremen" who knew plenty about yachting. I had to sit up with the boat all day to make sure they didn't sneak under the container for a peek.'

When high winds in the Pacific damaged the shrinkwrap plastic coating over the hull, Wallace tore it off and stuffed it around the base of the plywood case surrounding the keel. Anyone wanting to take a photograph had to break the container padlock and then wade through a mass of tangled plastic. No one bothered. John Longley had gone on to Newport in advance to arrange for the building of a special plywood security screen. 'The idea', he said, 'was simply to stop American designers from taking the very accurate photographs which might have allowed them to copy the wing. We never intended to take it any further. But when we saw how effective the idea of the green canvas skirts was, we decided to go the whole hog.'

In fact Newport Offshore did not have the security skirt ready on time so for two days after *Australia II* arrived in Newport on 26 May she sat in the water, a perfect target for photographers. Ben believes it may have been at this time that the photographs he later discovered tacked up behind a toilet door in the Canadian crewhouse were taken. The American sailmaker, Lowell North, who was closely associated with the defending *Courageous* syndicate, told me he had seen photographs of the keel. In Ben's view: 'The Yanks couldn't take the risk of being caught under the keel themselves but if the Canadians were caught, well that didn't matter so much. The New York Yacht Club thought that if they couldn't get rid of us easily, then they would get us eliminated and there was, early on, a feeling in Newport that *Canada 1* would prove to be a good boat. I think the Americans really believed that if they could only give *Canada 1* a little help they

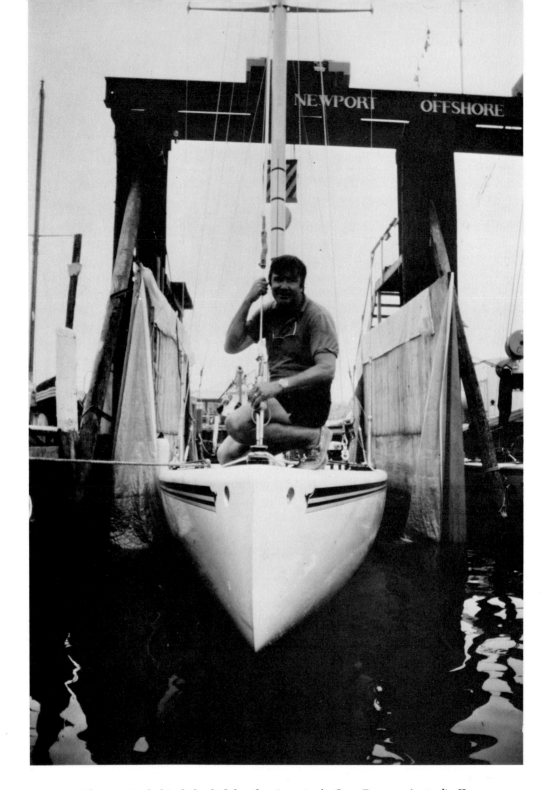

The genius behind the bid for the America's Cup: Ben on *Australia II*

might be able to beat us. They backed the wrong horse. They should have been helping *Challenge 12*.'

Australia II's reputation had preceded her. The Americans knew from the outset that they would be dealing with a radical, not to say revolutionary, yacht. And yet, despite all their experience in 12-metre and corporate campaigning, the New York Yacht Club allowed itself to be fooled by the Australians. Under the rules they were entitled to attend when the International Measurement Committee (chairman Tony Watts from England, Australia's John Savage and the American Mark Vinbury) met to conduct the official measurement at the Cove Haven Marina at Barrington near Newport. Bus Mosbacher claims that they did not attend because they had been advised that Alan Bond had posted armed guards around the shed in which *Australia II* was locked. The guards apparently had orders not to let anyone in: 'At the time we didn't much like the idea of facing down a guy with a gun. The Australians made it plain that they did not want us there, so we weren't about to push our luck with guards who had orders to keep us out. In retrospect it seems they were bluffing but at the time it certainly seemed serious to us.'

The keel remained shrouded in its green canvas cover and the deeper the mystery of its wings grew, the more determined the NYYC became to uncover what it felt certain was an unfair or rule-cheating device. Ben describes the hiding of the keel as if it were a schoolboy prank that had got out of hand: 'No one planned it. It just happened. And, of course, the more the Americans wanted to see it, the more we wanted to hide it. Their desperation was what made us hide it in the end. At first it was a joke but then they started getting really paranoid and so we decided, we'll hide the bloody thing for ever. I used to say that if we won the cup, we still wouldn't show them. We would just take it away and they'd never know what they raced against.' The Americans believed that they had a legitimate complaint from the outset but their handling of the situation proved disastrous.

The combination of the New York Yacht Club's apparent disregard for public opinion and the skilful exploitation of this by the Australians, recreated in people's minds the familiar images of Wall Street moguls and establishment blackcoats bearing down on a bunch of innocent sportsmen from down under. Rightly or wrongly this was the impression which the public was given throughout the competition. When *Australia II* finally beat *Victory 83* for the right to challenge, she was greeted by an incredible armada of spectator craft. Hundreds of ordinary Americans had turned out to show their personal solidarity with the Aussie underdog.

On 21 July 1983, eleven days before the NYYC made its first official protest against *Australia II*'s winged keel, I wrote and broadcast a report that the Americans were initiating moves which could lead to the eventual disqualification of the Australian boat. There was an attempt by some NYYC members to involve the

British in a protest over the wing. Whether through naïvety or ignorance the Americans failed to understand the very close personal ties that existed between the British syndicate chairman, Peter de Savary, and the *Australia II* syndicate chief, Alan Bond. De Savary and Bond were fierce competitors at sea and yet ashore they often met privately, dined aboard each other's yachts and shared information. Bondy and Peter de Savary were peas from the same pod. Both were self-made men and proud of the fact that they had come up the hard way. They were, as it turned out, natural allies in what would be a very fierce battle with the New York Yacht Club.

The same day that I reported the likelihood of the American challenge to *Australia II*'s keel, Alan Bond told me that he had information on the NYYC's activities which would 'shock the world'. 'New evidence', he said, 'has come to light on the extent to which the NYYC is prepared to go to secure a win by any means.' Bond was referring to attempts by Ed du Moulin, the *Freedom–Liberty* campaign manager, to buy the secrets of the *Australia II* keel for his own boats. With a perfect sense of timing Bond was to hold on to the du Moulin cable and the reply sent by the Dutch and use them to his own advantage at a full-scale press conference a week later.

On 31 July the NYYC dropped a bombshell. Former NYYC Commodore Bob McCullough, the chairman of the club's America's Cup Committee, walked into *Australia II*'s headquarters on the Newport waterfront to hand-deliver a three-page letter setting out the American case against the mystery keel. The nub of the allegations was that the keel had been unfairly rated. The club maintained that the keel's wingtips – which, it said, flared outwards and down from the bottom of the keel – gave the Australian boat the benefit of increased draft which had not been taken into consideration in her rating. If it had, the club claimed, *Australia II* would rate not at 12 metres but at 12.76 metres. *Australia II* would, the club maintained, be liable to incur a significant penalty in the sail area that it was allowed to carry.

According to McCullough's letter, the keel question arose under rule 27, which says in part:

> If from any peculiarity in the build of the yacht, or other cause, the measurer shall be of the opinion that the rule will not rate the yacht fairly, or that in any respect she does not comply with the requirements of these rules, he shall report the circumstances to the national authority . . . which, after due inquiry, shall award such certificate of rating as they may consider equitable and the measurement shall be deemed incomplete until this has been done.

McCullough's letter stated:

> There can be no question but that *Australia II* keel appendages are 'a peculiarity', which by dictionary definition is the quality or state of being different from

the normal. No 12-metre yacht and probably no other yacht anywhere, has had such appendages on her keel. Conclusive proof of the 'peculiarity' is afforded by the fact that the owners of *Australia II* have gone to unusual, albeit questionable, lengths to maintain complete secrecy as to the exact character and dimensions of the appendages. It is not necessary to delve into the niceties of measuring the yacht while heeled. The fact remains, in any event, that when the yacht heels, she gains unmeasured drafts. It goes without saying that the resulting increases in draft, lateral plane and stability are of material benefit and advantage to *Australia II*.

All this, McCullough said, led the America's Cup Committee to the 'inescapable conclusion' that *Australia II* was unfairly rated. The Australians took the challenge, which could have had them disqualified, with extraordinary calmness. Warren Jones, *Australia II*'s executive director and the man who deserves the lion's share of the credit for holding the crew together during the controversy, told me: 'We have got to make sure we've got our high ground guarded. And when we get on the high ground, those on the low ground are going to be in big trouble.' Jones was right.

He telephoned Bond in London and asked, 'Well, Bondy, what do you think?'

Bond replied: 'Let's do what we normally do pretty well. Let's fight.'

And they did.

Despite Jones' calm exterior he was very angry: 'They were contesting the boat on the grounds of "peculiarity". The only peculiar thing about *Australia II* is that she's bloody fast. They don't like that. They forget that in 1967 they introduced a revolutionary yacht named *Intrepid*. She had a trim tab on the back of her keel, she had a free-hanging rudder, she had a skeg and a bustle, and when you put her on the hard against good old *Dame Pattie* from Australia, that's when you saw something peculiar. She was peculiar. She was fast. But they owned her. That's the difference.'

Ben was his usual laconic self. His initial reaction was 'no reaction'. 'We always get something every time we come here,' he said. 'In 1974 they asked questions about *Southern Cross*'s rudder. Last time, 1980, they made a fuss over our bendy mast. So all this is just normal America's Cup stuff. They think it's illegal because it's fast and could possibly beat them. I'm not worried about it. I don't think it is illegal and nor do the International Measurement Committee. When they measured the boat, not one of them raised the point that it was peculiar or different.' Ben was right. There had been no complaint from the committee when they awarded the boat a 12-metre rating certificate, thus making her legal. That consensus did not change, although the American measurer, Mark Vinbury, made it clear much later on that he did have his own doubts about the 'fairness in equity' of *Australia II*'s rating.

At the start of the controversy Ben wanted to go straight to the International Yacht Racing Union for a resolution. Warren Jones, recognizing that this was what the Americans wanted, was determined not to give way. He felt that to go to the IYRU would be seen as an admission of defeat. A shrewd tactician, he argued that while the NYYC were worried about the keel they were not campaigning their boats. Ben describes Warren as 'sparring' with the New York Yacht Club. As the fight became more vicious and the club turned its attack on Ben his health began to suffer. Yvonne Lexcen remembers Ben's depression and blinding headaches. 'He couldn't believe those NYYC people were saying those things about him. We never knew what incredible stories they were going to come up with next. It really hurt him.' Ben's blood pressure went shooting up and he suffered from terrible pains in the chest and the neck – the symptoms of an imminent heart attack. When he went to a doctor in Newport, the leads on the cardiogram were put on to him the wrong way round and he was diagnosed as having had a massive heart attack. Rushed into hospital, at the cost of $5,000 for one week, it was discovered that he was merely suffering from high blood pressure. Yvonne thinks that going into hospital was good for Ben because it forced him to rest. 'He bounced back after that. I think he made up his mind in hospital that he wasn't going to allow the NYYC to get on top of him. Ben is very courageous but he's also very sensitive. All those allegations hurt him. I don't think he could ever forgive them for that.'

Rarely, if ever, in the stormy history of the world's oldest continuous sporting event, had two supposedly 'friendly' competitors been so openly at each other's throats. The polite fiction that the America's Cup had something to do with sport seemed to vanish beneath a bitter sea of recriminations and anger. It was, to use the Australian vernacular, 'on for young and old'. Clearly the NYYC sensed that in *Australia II* it faced a yacht that was at last capable of winning sport's most coveted prize. The spectre of defeat had been 132 years in arriving, but there it sat, a long white yacht with green-and-gold cove stripes and a bounding green kangaroo on its bows. Wrapped in a green canvas shroud, *Australia II* was guarded day and night; some of the men carried guns. Alan Bond came close to the truth when he said: 'This is not sport. It's war.'

Warren Jones sought solemn promises from each of the three international measurers that they would not disclose the yacht's vital statistics, nor allow themselves to, as he put it, 'buckle under pressure from the Americans'. Mark Vinbury soon wished he had never laid eyes on the winged keel. Ben claimed that the American syndicates hounded Vinbury day and night trying to find out what the keel was like. Vinbury had told him that viewing the keel was 'like seeing some holy relic that you're not supposed to speak about or your tongue burns out'. When key measurements from the *Australia II* keel turned up in NYYC documents, journalist Hugh McIlvanney was bold enough to comment in the *Observer* that the Australians were busy looking for scorch marks around the mouths of certain measurers.

One of the more absurd ironies of the keel controversy was that early in July 1983 senior members of the NYYC were seriously considering building a 12-metre yacht with a keel very similar to the one it now claimed was illegal. Russell Long, the young man who had done such a good job with the *Clipper* campaign in 1980, put together a scheme to buy the discarded *Magic*, designed by Johan Valentijn, hack her off at deck level and completely rebuild her underbody along the supposed lines of *Australia II*. The NYYC was reported to be enthusiastic, but Dennis Conner, the man they would eventually rely on to drive their cup defender, *Liberty*, was not. Conner reasoned that such an effort would be a waste of time and money which could be better spent toning the existing cup defence candidate. Conner prevailed and the idea was dropped, leaving the Americans to watch with growing awe as Australia notched up a staggering and indeed unprecedented forty-one wins with only six losses at the end of the finals.

The NYYC made its next move against the keel on 4 August when it sent a weighty legal petition to the International Yacht Racing Union asking for an immediate ruling on the matter. This time the NYYC's petition included a letter written by Mark Vinbury to the IYRU's chief measurer, Tony Watts. In the letter Vinbury said that he felt Ben Lexcen should have informed the measurers of the theoretical advantages of the keel, which were not taxed under the 12-metre rule. Vinbury's letter was cited as Exhibit A and was just one of twelve documents written by some of America's most distinguished yachtsmen. Significant by its absence, however, was the name Olin Stephens, the doyen of American naval architects and the man who, through his six cup defenders, had done more than anyone else to keep the cup in American hands.

Ben still maintains an almost awestruck respect for Olin Stephens. In fact he continues to see Stephens, the man he calls 'God', as the measure by which every designer should gauge his success. Ben always wanted to work with Sparkman and Stephens in New York but he says he was afraid they would turn him down because he lacked any real training. 'I would have been happy just sharpening the pencils and packing up the place after closing time.' In the middle of all the furore over the winged keel, Olin Stephens emerged from the privacy of his retirement in Putney, Vermont, to pronounce the winged keel concept a genuine and legitimate breakthrough in 12-metre design. He offered his personal congratulations to Ben Lexcen for having solved with his winged keel, one of the truly vexed questions of modern yachting design, that is control of the energy-sapping tip-vortex. Ben was elated almost to the point of tears. 'God had spoken', he said, 'and delivered His blessing.'

When Alan Bond came ashore on the night of 4 August after a long day at sea he was almost white with rage. He accused the NYYC of having a 'paranoiac attitude' towards *Australia II*. 'Fortunately,' he said, 'we race under international rules and not rules set up for the benefit of one club. While yachting has an international body that administers it, we are quite satisfied that all will be well.'

The tone and language of the NYYC letters, if not paranoiac, was certainly angry. In the letter to the acting chairman of the IYRU's Keelboat Committee, James Michael, a member of the NYYC's America's Cup Committee, claimed that it had been impossible to present the evidence at an earlier time because the *Australia II* syndicate had gone to 'unusual and highly questionable lengths to maintain complete secrecy concerning the keel and its appendages'. Michael claimed that those measures included shrouding the yacht's underbody when hauled from the water; using electronically charged screens around her berth; having the yacht measured in a closed shed to which access was barred by armed guards; swearing the measurers to keep secret the shape and dimensions; and round-the-clock security guards. He went on to say that the degree to which *Australia II* was not 'fairly rated' could not be conclusively demonstrated until she had sailed in a representative number of races. In the light of this, the America's Cup Committee had come to the following 'inescapable conclusions':

1   The appendages to the keel of *Australia II* constitute a peculiarity within the meaning and intent of the rules.

2   The appendages give the yacht decided benefits and advantages, as witness her performance record.

3   The appendages are either illegal under the rating rule, or, at the very least, are not fairly rated thereunder.

4   Therefore, it was required that the Keelboat Committee awarded such certificate of rating as is 'equitable'.

American naval architect Halsey Herreshoff came to the point rather more succinctly when he wrote: 'If the closely guarded, peculiar keel design of *Australia II* is allowed to remain in the competition or is allowed to continue to be rated without penalty, the yacht will likely win the foreign trials and will likely win the America's Cup in September 1983.'

Two days later, on 7 August, three of the NYYC's most senior officials sought a private meeting with Alan Bond at his Newport home – Midcliff. Commodores Robert Stone and Bob McCullough with Vice-Commodore Bus Mosbacher met Bond and Warren Jones for two hours. 'It was', said Warren Jones, 'like two brick walls sitting opposite each other in the lounge room.' According to Bus Mosbacher, Bond had yelled at them and made a scene. 'We were trying to be civil,' he said. 'He was threatening to drag our name through the mud.' So the two sides parted, almost certainly more bitterly divided than before.

In the meantime letters and cables of condemnation and scorn aimed at the NYYC were piling up at both the club's headquarters and at the *Australia II* dockside office. The Australian waterfront headquarters looked like the inside of a drover's hut with bits of paper tacked up all over the walls. A telegram from a man in California castigated the NYYC for what he called its '*Australia II* rhubarb'. He went on to advise them 'for the sake of yachting and good sportsmanship . . . to quit bellyaching and go sailing'. Other cables reflected similar unrest in America's heartland: 'Let Australia sail as is and beat them or lose with no complaints like Jack Dempsey did when he "forgot to duck". Win this way and you will win international admiration. The Mid West feels this way.'

The keel controversy was also upsetting the challengers. The Aga Khan, head of the Italian challenge syndicate, thought: 'The controversy over the keel puts the semi-finalists in a much more difficult position. The challengers don't really know where they stand any more.' He stated that the challengers had a right to know whether Australia did or did not qualify as a 12-metre before they resumed racing in the semi-finals. Dr Beppe Croce, the IYRU president, seemed at this time to endorse the Australian stand. He repeated the view that the winged keel was merely a 'development'. 'The 12-metre class is a development class,' he told me, 'so it is logical that there should be improvements with every new boat.'

On 10 August, ten days after the American allegations had surfaced, Vice-Commodore Bus Mosbacher broke the long and strained silence. Mosbacher claimed the NYYC's position had been misunderstood and misrepresented. In a long interview in the University Club in New York, he told me that the NYYC was not saying that the Australian keel was illegal: 'We are not protesting the keel. We are not saying the measurement is in error. What we are saying is that it is an unusual, new and innovative development for the 12-metre class and as such it should be cleared by the IYRU's Keelboat Committee, the sport's supreme court.'

Mosbacher, still using the title ambassador, bestowed on him during his years as President Nixon's Chief of Protocol, was as polished and persuasive as his rank suggests. He set out the NYYC's case clearly and with disarming logic: 'This is not an in-house protest at all. We are seeking a clarification, for the Keelboat Committee to take a look at it. To say either yes, it's fine, or no, it should be rated in another way. We are perfectly willing to have stated that we want to abide by their decision whatever it may be. We have tried to keep this as fair and as equitable as possible, as we believe it is our responsibility to do.'

He rejected charges that the NYYC had sought to 'waive the rules in order to rule the waves'. While admitting, 'It is true the rules have been changed over the past 100 years of cup competition', he insisted that: 'Every single one of those changes has been made to benefit the challengers, not the NYYC. If we wanted to we could have accepted only one challenger this year instead of ten, of whom seven carried through.'

On the following day, 11 August, the International Measurement Committee reaffirmed by a unanimous vote that *Australia II* was a legal 12-metre. Mark Vinbury who was also the NYYC's official measurer, differed from his two colleagues when they agreed that racing rule 27 did not apply in the case of *Australia II's* keel. As far as the Australians were concerned this should have laid the matter to rest but within an hour of the measurers' statement the NYYC responded. They issued their own statement saying that the measurers' pronouncement only increased the urgency for an immediate ruling by the Keelboat Committee. The NYYC seemed oblivious to the fact that the International Measurement Committee's chairman, Tony Watts, was also the IYRU's chief measurer. Relations between Watts and the America's Cup committee men were extremely strained. Some of the NYYC's most senior members expressed the private view that he was 'on the Australians' side'. Tony Watts is a man whose judgement and integrity are well known. It is an indication of the NYYC's desperation that they should doubt one of the most honest men in yachting. Watts was privately dismayed but felt constrained to say nothing.

On 14 August the NYYC campaign to disqualify *Australia II's* keel took a bizarre twist. Warren Jones, having carefully bided his time, released two devastating telex messages which showed what he described as 'the kind of deception and double dealing the Americans are up to'. One of the telexes was addressed to Dr Peter Van Oossanen, the Director of Research and Development at the Netherlands Ship Model Basin in Wageningen and was from Ed du Moulin, manager of the *Freedom–Liberty* cup campaign. Du Moulin was asking for help in building a keel identical to that which the NYYC was trying to have outlawed.

> I understand that you and your team are responsible for development and design of a special keel for *Australia II*. We are finally convinced of her potential and would, therefore, like to build same design under one of our boats. We will keep this confidential so as not to jeopardize your agreement with Alan Bond. However, due to complexity of problems, need your maximum effort and experience. We can start next week and be ready by 25 August. Please telex your design and consultancy fees and any other conditions which might apply. An immediate reply is of utmost importance.

Jones then produced a second telex, the reply to du Moulin's cable from the Netherlands Ship Model Basin:

> We have received your telex addressed to attention to our Dr Van Oossanen, and would ask you to note firstly that we were associated with the *Australia II* campaign by way of a tank-testing contract. Their designer, Mr Ben Lexcen, resided at Wageningen for four months whilst he completed the designs for both *Australia II* and *Challenge 12*. As we are contracted to them not to test

12-metre models for any other 12-metre syndicate until the completion of the 1983 campaign, we have today advised them of your query and requested their permission to undertake work for you. But unfortunately they have advised us that they are not prepared to allow such dispensation.

Both telexes were attached to a long and detailed legal argument from Warren Jones to IYRU president, Dr Beppe Croce. Jones, a self-confessed 'corporate brawler', relished the cut and thrust of the battle with the NYYC, especially as he appeared to be winning. With righteous indignation he argued that the American efforts to buy and install the Australian-designed keel on an American yacht in time for the cup finals appeared to be in direct contravention of the NYYC's own 1982 resolution which requires that each competitor's boat must be designed by nationals of that country. He pointed out how curious it seemed to the Australians that the leading yacht in the defenders' trials had tried to purchase the Australian keel design, while the NYYC were attempting to have the design re-rated by incurring a penalty. Jones said that the telex evidence raised serious questions concerning the NYYC's good faith in mounting its request for reconsideration of *Australia II*'s rating. The NYYC's latest statement announced that the club had only recently become aware of the details of the *Australia II* keel and Jones was quick to pounce on this:

> We would like to know where these details were obtained, since it is common knowledge that we keep all details of our boat secret. If the NYYC is in receipt of specific information it can only be through improper means and we have the right to know who passed it to them and under what conditions.

The Australians never pressed this point but at a subsequent press conference Jones disclosed that Peter de Savary had been approached in London by an unknown man who claimed that for £50,000 he could sell him detailed plans of *Australia II*'s winged keel, which had apparently been stolen from Ben Lexcen's Sydney office.

Having issued their statement the NYYC's committee members had sailed off on a cruise along the coast of Maine. In what the Australians regarded as typically arrogant style the New Yorkers remained incommunicado for over a week. The NYYC had set about their protest with all the finesse of a bull charging at a gate. Instead of going through the proper channels and using the United States Yacht Racing Union (USYRU) as a vehicle, they rushed to send their own communications direct to the IYRU in London. When the IYRU reminded them that it did not deal with clubs but only with national bodies, the USYRU intervened with objections which were, of course, similar to those of the NYYC. This flurry of paperwork caused the IYRU to schedule a special meeting in London where its most senior members could consider the request that the keel be examined by the all-powerful

Keelboat Committee. The meeting, which was set for 30 August, never took place.

While the New York Yacht Club protested, Peter de Savary was waiting on the sidelines before making a sensational disclosure. Finally, on 21 August, de Savary and Bond called the press conference that cut the ground from under the NYYC. De Savary had in his possession a letter revealing that the Keelboat Committee had given his designer, Ian Howlett, clearance to use winged appendages. In Ben's view de Savary was the only one of the foreign challengers who came out of the keel affair with his sense of honour intact. 'It was in his interest to keep quiet about the letter. He liked the idea of having us under pressure. The IYRU guys who did know simply said that someone had already been given a ruling on winglets by the Keelboat Committee. They couldn't say who it was. But then somebody told Bondy that Peter had a letter and we went to ask him if it was true. And he said yes. He said he would send Kit Hobday round with it in an hour but he insisted on making the announcement to the press himself. We had suspected that he had the letter for about a week but we thought that he wouldn't tell us.'

Peter de Savary released details from Ian Howlett's confidential correspondence with IYRU chief measurer, Tony Watts. Howlett had asked Watts three questions: Are winglets permitted on the keel? May these be adjusted in trim? May they be restricted? Watts had replied that a quorum of the Keelboat Committee had decided that winglets were permitted so long as the static draft was not exceeded. He said that adjustment of the angle of incidence was not allowed and that the winglets could not be retracted. De Savary, who sat up on the dais with Alan Bond at the press conference, concluded that these interpretations of the 12-metre rule proved to him that the winged keel concept was legal. This, of course, was enthusiastically endorsed by Bond.

It was at that point that Ken Weller, a senior official of the USYRU, asked Bond when he had learned of the interpretation. When Bond snapped the answer 'today', Weller pointed out that the keel had been entered in the competition without any knowledge of the IYRU opinion. Bond, glaring down from the dais, told Weller that he did not intend to answer any more of his questions. The American designer, Gary Mull, then stood up and identified himself as a member of the Keelboat Committee. 'It is', he said, 'the policy of the Keelboat Committee to announce all rule interpretations each November to the public. My question to Mr de Savary is: does he know of any reason why this interpretation was not made public last November?' De Savary replied that he did not and an ashen-faced Bond reached for the microphone to request that Mull leave the meeting: 'I think, Mr Mull, that you have demonstrated that you are biased on this question. It is therefore improper that you should be here.' Mull walked out.

Outside the press conference Mull continued to ask why Tony Watts had not disclosed details of his correspondence with Howlett. 'The Keelboat Committee has an announced policy of not allowing secret rule interpretations, and since this letter came in July 1982, I would just like to know why the interpretation was not made public. In November I specifically asked Tony Watts for all 12-metre interpretations and I didn't get anything on this.' This question was never answered satisfactorily. Peter de Savary subsequently claimed that it was simply a matter of confidentiality between Howlett and Watts.

The next day, 22 August, I was invited aboard NYYC Vice-Commodore Bus Mosbacher's motor yacht, *Summertime.* There I was introduced to the chairman of the America's Cup Committee, Commodore Bob McCullough and the committee's secretary, Vic Romagna. The three men then gave me the first details of the NYYC's investigations in the Netherlands. They were very concerned at reports in the Dutch press, specifically in the *Amsterdam Telegraaf,* which made serious allegations that it was a team of Dutch scientists, and not Ben Lexcen, who had designed *Australia II.* If the claims were true, Mosbacher said, then the club would have to pursue them: 'I know Ben Lexcen and I have the greatest respect for him, but if in fact he's not the sole designer, or at least if there is a major contribution to the design of the boat by non-Australians, then that is contrary to the Deed of Gift and the Conditions of Match.' Mosbacher then declined to say what the consequences might be if the Dutch reports should prove accurate, but plainly there could only be one course of action and that was disqualification. Commodore McCullough told me later that the club would not have flinched in pressing disqualification proceedings before the international jury.

On 23 August I had long telephone conversations with Dr Peter Van Oossanen and his superior Dr Oosterveld at the Netherlands Ship Model Basin and also with Dr Joop Sloof. Van Oossanen said that he had been visited by three men from the NYYC who had tried to extract what he called a 'confession' from him. 'When they came to see me,' he told me, 'they made it clear in a none too subtle way that they expected me to own up and confess that the keel was really a Dutch invention. I told them, "Don't be ridiculous. This is Ben Lexcen's keel," but they didn't seem to want to believe what I said.' They had told Van Oossanen that they were convinced that the self-taught Lexcen, with no formal degree in naval architecture, could not possibly have conceived and designed a keel concept as sophisticated as the delta-winged device at the base of *Australia II*'s keel. The Netherlands Ship Model Basin is 50 per cent owned by the Dutch government and the NYYC delegation, in trying to bring pressure to bear on Van Oossanen, told him that they had taken their case to the highest levels in the Dutch Ministry of Public Works. Dr Van Oossanen maintained that Lexcen was in charge throughout the four months he had tested the designs in the Netherlands. When the delegation went to visit Dr Joop Sloof at the Dutch National Aerospace Laboratories they confronted him with the same allegations. 'Dr Sloof', said Dr Oossanen, 'told them he had collaborated with Ben Lexcen in testing the wings for *Australia II,* but once again he told them that he simply conducted the computer testing of Lexcen's design ideas.'

On 24 August I spoke to Dr Van Oossanen immediately after the NYYC delegation had left his office. He had been with Richard Latham, a senior member of the America's Cup Committee, and Will Valentijn, the uncle of *Liberty*'s designer, Johan Valentijn, for over an hour and a half. At the meeting, he said, they had tried to make him sign an affidavit discrediting Lexcen's claim to be the sole designer of *Australia II*. Dr Van Oossanen felt that: 'It was a clear attempt to manufacture evidence against Ben Lexcen. Most of the assertions in the statement were wrong. They clearly wanted to discredit Ben so that they could disqualify *Australia II* and eliminate the threat it posed to the America's Cup. I told them: "No, definitely not. There's no way I'll sign anything like that. It's just not true." '

The Americans had first presented Dr Joop Sloof with a document to sign on 9 August. They were insistent that he should take full credit for the work he had done on the Australian keel. Joop Sloof said to them: 'No, my work was as a tester of Ben Lexcen's ideas. He is the one who designed this, not me.' The Americans did not want to believe this and so they put pressure on Sloof's director, Mr Verbano, but to no avail.

Ben thought that the 'country of origin' rule for the America's Cup match was senseless. He does not believe that national independence can exist in a multinational research environment: 'Does Johan Valentijn listen to his old professor when he goes to Holland to tank-test? Of course he does. The designer can't say to himself, "Oh, I didn't hear that." I have a Japanese computer that I use with an American program; my pocket calculator is from somewhere else. Can we use those tools? The tank-testing computer facilities in Holland were tools. I taught them the mechanics of testing yachts with really big models and they taught me how to make sense out of the test data.' He found the allegations extremely upsetting: 'They are accusing me of cheating. The same guys who raced an incredibly illegal boat in 1974, *Courageous*, are standing up and telling the world that my boat isn't mine. I have a mind to admit it all and tell them that I really owe the secret of the design to a Greek guy who helped me out. He's been dead for 2,000 years but he's been invaluable. Bloody Archimedes.'

Meanwhile, the Australians back in Newport were preparing the move that would put an end to the nagging question of the legality of *Australia II*'s keel. They had obtained a facsimile of Tony Watts' confidential letter to Ian Howlett. The day after Warren Jones handed Bob McCullough the facsimile the NYYC conceded defeat. The club had always maintained that it would abide by the umpire's decision. Now that that decision had at last been made, they accepted it with public good grace although privately they felt bitterly disappointed and bewildered. For the first time in cup history it appeared that America would face an opponent with a radically different hull, one that was a proven light-air champion and one that could conceivably end their proud boast to hold the longest winning streak in the history of sport.

Just before the start of the America's Cup series on 13 September there was to be yet one more twist in the winged keel controversy. The NYYC's attorney, James Michael, drew up a three-page 'Certificate of Compliance', an affidavit which the committee wanted the Australians to sign. On 11 September, the day before the America's Cup captains' meeting, Bob McCullough presented the document to Alan Bond. It set out in ten very legalistic points, all the darkest assumptions the committee had been making about the illegality of *Australia II*'s winged keel:

CERTIFICATION OF COMPLIANCE WITH THE CONDITIONS GOVERNING THE RACES FOR THE AMERICA'S CUP 1983

Whereas: AUSTRALIA II, representing the Royal Perth Yacht Club, has won the elimination races held between the several challenging yachts, and

Whereas: the Royal Perth Yacht Club and the America's Cup Challenge 1983, Limited, (herein the 'AUSTRALIA II Syndicate') desire to obtain the agreement of the New York Yacht Club to the substitution of the Royal Perth Yacht Club as the Challenging Club and the acceptance of AUSTRALIA II as the Challenger; and

Whereas: such agreement and acceptance by the New York Yacht Club are conditioned upon assurances satisfactory to it that the substituted challenging club and substituted challenger have heretofore complied, and will in the future comply, in all respects with the Conditions Governing the Races for the America's Cup 1983, as required by Section 16 thereof; and

Whereas: Section 12 of said conditions provides that AUSTRALIA II shall comply in every respect with the requirements regarding construction, sails and equipment in the Deed of Gift of the America's Cup, dated October 24, 1887, the 1958 Resolution, the 1980 Resolutions, the Footnotes in Amplification thereof and the Further Amplification of the 1980 Resolution, dated January 30, 1981, (copies of each of which are attached hereto) applying to national origin of design and construction; and

Whereas: information available to the New York Yacht Club has raised certain questions regarding AUSTRALIA II's compliance with said Section 12, as to which the Royal Perth Yacht Club, the AUSTRALIA II Syndicate and the designer of AUSTRALIA II desire to provide such clarifications and assurances as will insure that the New York Yacht Club has fulfilled its obligation, as trustee under the Deed of Gift, to wit, 'that it will faithfully and fully see that the foregoing conditions are fully observed and complied with by any contestant for the said Cup'.

NOW THEREFORE, the undersigned Peter R. Dalziell, Commodore, for and on behalf of the Royal Perth Yacht Club; Alan Bond, Chairman, and Warren Jones, Executive Director, each for and on behalf of the AUSTRALIA II Syndicate; and Ben Lexcen, designer of AUSTRALIA II, in order to provide such clarifications and assurances and to gain the aforesaid agreement and acceptance by the New York Yacht Club, do hereby jointly and severally, make the following representations, certifications and warranties to the New York Yacht Club:

1. AUSTRALIA II was designed solely and exclusively by Ben Lexcen, a national of Australia, and no 'foreign consultants' and no 'foreign designer—however he is designated' assisted or participated in the design of AUSTRALIA II's keel, hull, rig or sails.

2. All tank tests leading to the design of AUSTRALIA II, conducted in the Netherlands Ship Model Basin, were under the sole supervision of Australian nationals and the designs were from the drawing board of Australian nationals, in accordance with the letter of June 11, 1982 from the America's Cup Committee to the AUSTRALIA II Syndicate, a copy of which is attached hereto.

3. Neither the AUSTRALIA II Syndicate nor Ben Lexcen contracted with or retained the Netherlands Ship Model Basin to perform consulting and research services to assist in the design of AUSTRALIA II. Neither the Netherlands Ship Model Basin nor the Netherlands National Aerospace Laboratory, or any employee or representative of either of said organizations, contributed any inventions or design concepts which led to or were incorporated in the design of the keel, hull and/or rig of AUSTRALIA II.

4. The only computer programs employed at the Netherlands Ship Model Basin, in connection with the design of AUSTRALIA II, were standard computer programs used at that facility to evaluate the results of tank tests of models from the drawing board of Australian nationals. No proprietary or confidential computer programs were developed for or made available to Ben Lexcen or the AUSTRALIA II Syndicate for use in developing by computer the design of the keel, hull and/or rig of AUSTRALIA II.

5. The keel design of AUSTRALIA II, on which Ben Lexcen filed on February, 1982 patent application number 8200457 with the Netherlands Patent Office, was totally and solely conceived by Ben Lexcen, and neither the Netherlands Ship Model Basin nor the Netherlands National Aerospace Laboratory, or any employee or representative of either of said organizations, participated in or contributed to the invention.

6. The hull of AUSTRALIA II was constructed and built entirely in Australia, including the lofting and the fabrication and assembling of all framing and plating.

7. The spars of AUSTRALIA II were manufactured in the United States using standard extrusions; however, all the engineering and design details of the taper and scarf splice, as well as all other fittings, shroud positions, spreader

details, etc., were provided by Ben Lexcen, in accordance with the America's Cup Committee's letter of January 13, 1983 to all Challengers, a copy of which is attached hereto.

8. Any computers or other electronic equipment carried aboard AUSTRALIA II to monitor her performance were either designed and manufactured by Australian nationals or are standard 'shelf items' generally available; and no such equipment was either custom designed or custom built by other than nationals of Australia.

9. AUSTRALIA II, the AUSTRALIA II Syndicate and the Royal Perth Yacht Club have, and each of them has, complied, and will in the future comply, in all respects with the Conditions Governing the Races for the America's Cup 1983.

10. Each of the undersigned further declares, under penalty of perjury, that each of the foregoing representations, certifications and warranties is true and correct.

Dated: at Newport, Rhode Island, September _____, 1983

Peter R. Dalziell, Commodore, for and on behalf of the Royal Perth Yacht Club	Warren Jones, Executive Director, for and on behalf of the America's Cup Challenge 1983, Limited (AUSTRALIA II Syndicate)
Alan Bond, Chairman, for and on behalf of the America's Cup Challenge 1983 Limited (AUSTRALIA II Syndicate)	Ben Lexcen, Designer of AUSTRALIA II

If the Australians had agreed to sign the affidavit, they would have been declaring publicly, and under penalty of perjury, that they had complied with the 'Conditions' governing the races. Bond refused.

McCullough's next step was to go to Bill Fesq, the distinguished former Commodore of the Royal Sydney Yacht Squadron, who was acting as liaison chairman for all the challengers. He is reported to have demanded that Fesq 'find another challenger'. Fesq, who had come up against the NYYC before, when *Gretel II* was disqualified against *Intrepid* in the 1970 America's Cup, refused to consider any other challenger.

On 12 September the America's Cup Committee met aboard Mosbacher's *Summertime*, just two hours before the historic captains' meeting. Michael Levitt and Barbara Lloyd in their book *Upset* described this meeting at which the committee members were still convinced of the cheating allegation: 'but they had run out of time and the question before them that day on *Summertime* was whether to let the whole thing drop or keep pressing. In fact, the decision to be made was whether to proceed with a match between *Liberty* and *Australia II* or cancel the America's Cup races.'

The committee certainly had the power to cancel the cup. But at what an enormous cost. Seven challengers had been campaigning in Newport all summer and tens of millions of dollars had already been spent on the event. To stop it all now would mean risking the kind of international uproar that even the NYYC could not ignore. 'We were in a tight spot,' Victor Romagna told Levitt and Lloyd with classic understatement. 'We didn't want to appear to be spoiling for it, but we were convinced the Australians had overlooked nearly every rule.'

A few members of the nine-man committee were absent but in the discussion that ensued everyone made his position clear. In Romagna's words: 'All of a sudden the discussion came to a shuddering halt. At that point, if we did vote it was clear that four members agreed to continue and five wanted to pull out.... We didn't have the guts to stand up and say, "We won't race." And so we just folded up our tents and went off into oblivion.' The America's Cup was saved, but the New York Yacht Club was not.

Chapter Six

America's Cup 1983: The Challenge

Race One
14 September
***Liberty* d. *Australia II* by 1 minute 10 seconds**

The first race was scheduled for Tuesday, 13 September. An enormous spectator fleet, variously estimated at between 1,500 and 2,000 vessels, trailed out of Newport across the slate-grey waters of Rhode Island Sound to surround the America's Cup buoy. It was the biggest fleet in the history of cup competition. Yachts big and small had come from all over the world bringing together men and women who sensed that they would be watching a historical race. The coastguard had thirty chase boats and half a dozen much larger boats but they were still not enough to keep the mob under control.

It was a glorious summer day, warm and sunny with a gentle north-easterly breeze, which promised ideal conditions for *Australia II*. In the air above the crowded sea helicopters whirred in a great clockwise circle and above them a bank of light aircraft droned through anti-clockwise loops. In the middle of them all, like a great silver bullet, serene and unaffected by all the turbulent whizzing and buzzing, sat the majestic silver blimp with its NYYC observer and a television camera crew.

Down behind the starting line stood the coastguard's glorious three-masted barque *Eagle*, and near her a US destroyer flying from either side of her bridge multicoloured code flags that signalled, 'Good luck *Liberty*. Good luck *Australia II*.' The NYYC's Race Committee vessel *Black Knight* took up her station ready for the

Tension aboard *Black Swan*, the Australian tender, during one of the cup races

12.10 p.m. start. Ben and Alan Bond watched the America's Cup races from the Australian tender, *Black Swan*. All *Australia II*'s instruments were duplicated on a console on the tender's bridge so that Bondy could, in a sense, sail aboard the challenger by 'remote control'. As Bond invariably took the most comfortable chair, Ben found himself leaping around between the bridge and a sort of nest he had fashioned down among the big blue plastic sail bags on the foredeck. 'Bondy knows the numbers,' Ben said. 'He was sitting up there watching shifts and urging the crew to "tack now" or "go left". If they'd done all the things Bondy said, they'd have won four-straight. It was hard to watch. It's always painful when you've got a big interest.'

At precisely 11.50 a.m. the Race Committee men, immaculate in Brenton red trousers, black jackets and white shirts and ties, hoisted the course signals that indicated that the bearing to the first mark would be 30°. The nor'-nor'-easter was blowing at no more than 8 knots. At noon the ten-minute warning gun boomed over Rhode Island Sound and the great racing yachts, one stark white and the other blood-red, came in together from either end of the line for the very first time. The armchair admirals had all predicted that there would be furious turning and wheeling from the moment they met, but Conner and Bertrand, the two skippers, proved them wrong.

There was a tentative circling as both crews sounded each other out. The

circling became a little more intense before the five-minute gun, but then, with just two minutes to the start, the red-and-white postponement flag went up aboard *Black Knight*. The tension was broken and both boats retired, like boxers, to their respective corners. The Race Committee has to satisfy itself that the breeze in which they start a race is not only a true one, but that its direction is at right angles to the first mark. They had recorded a 40° shift to the east, which meant that if they had started on time, it would have made the first leg into a reach instead of a beat to windward. The coastguard then had the monumental job of clearing the spectator boats away from the new course set as 90°.

Two hours later, at 1.50 p.m. the course signals went up. The countdown began at 2 p.m. and this time there was a lot more fire in the circling manoeuvres with *Australia II* clearly in command. We had seen *Australia II* in action against lesser boats for three months but here at last was proof positive that she had a significant edge on *Liberty*. She did not so much turn as pivot at the start where the object of all this circling is to dominate and control the rival boat. At 2.08 p.m. with two and a half minutes to the gun, a blue-and-white 'A' flag was hoisted with the postponement pennant. The 'A' signalled abandonment. This time the breeze had shifted 35° to east-south-east and the Race Committee, to-gether with Royal Perth Yacht Club's observer, John Fitzhardinge, decided that it was too late to try a third time. The enormous spectator fleet carried more than a few perplexed and disappointed passengers home to Newport that afternoon. The Australians agreed that the NYYC had done the right thing.

Wednesday, 14 September dawned cold and overcast. A north-easterly breeze (045°) was blowing a true 18 knots and there was a slight chop on the grey-green sea. Small craft were warned not to venture outside the sheltered waters of Narragansett Bay but they still came in a great waterborne caravan that swept from Castle Hill to the America's Cup buoy 7.2 miles to seaward. The conditions were said to be ideal for *Liberty* but *Australia II* surprised the Americans with her great stability and pointing ability.

The race, which was to be one of the most exciting match races ever sailed in 12-metre yachts, began on time. After a seemingly endless summer of trials the contest had been reduced to two superbly matched boats with crews drilled to perfection and sails to match. *Australia II* crossed the line three seconds ahead but with *Liberty* very close by to windward. *Australia II* was able to lee bow the defender and force Conner to tack away for clear air. In the bitterly cold breeze and the savage chop, it was difficult for either boat to settle. Conner and his tactician, Tom Whidden, stood on the right-hand side of the course on port tack. The American skipper could be seen hunched over the wheel in intense concen-tration, a big man with a streak of white suncream smeared across his lips and a bright red crash helmet clamped firmly on his head. The helmet was a precaution against the deadly force of free-swinging, running backstay blocks and the low

Australia II

angle of the aluminium boom. Conner and his crew were kitted out in dark blue uniform while the Australians wore their national colours, green-and-gold jerseys overlaid with white foul-weather gear.

After nine minutes *Liberty* tacked to starboard. As the two boats crossed tacks for the first time it was clear that the Australians were in front and a great war-whoop of joy went up from spectator boats festooned with green-and-gold ribbons. Bertrand immediately tacked on top of *Liberty*, forcing Conner to tack back to port to keep his air clear. He stood on into a slight header, tacked on to right of way starboard and gained a narrow lead the next time they crossed. Both boats sailed on on starboard with the Australians on the inside of a lift that enabled them to cross ahead of *Liberty* again, tack and then cover her closely right to the starboard layline. *Australia II* rounded eight seconds ahead amid the howls and whoops of support from Australian spectators. It was the first time in modern America's Cup history that a foreign challenger had led an American defender around the first mark. It was an omen of things to come.

As the Australians rounded the big, bright orange buoy her green-and-gold-striped tri-radial kite popped out like a perfect bubble. *Australia II* went racing off to the wing mark with *Liberty* hard on her heels under a red, white and blue striped chute. Conner tried to ease out on to *Australia II*'s windward quarter, threatening to project her wind shadow over the Australian boat. It did not work. But in maintaining their position the Australians were lulled into a false sense of security and Bertrand made an error which could conceivably have cost *Australia II* the race. Early on, on the first reaching leg Bertrand had watched with some satisfaction as *Liberty* tried and failed to sail up and over him. When Conner tried it again on the third leg Bertrand felt confident he couldn't do it again. This was a grave mistake. *Australia II* rounded the gybe mark ten seconds ahead but when Conner tried the same tactic on the port gybe they failed to respond quickly enough and soon Conner had the big red American boat riding up and through the Australian quarter wave. The Americans wore a beautiful flat-cut staysail beneath their spinnaker while the Australians only belatedly set theirs two-thirds of the way down the leg. Watching *Liberty* powering right over the top of *Australia II* was one of the most awe-inspiring sights of the entire cup summer.

Liberty rounded to the leeward mark twenty-six seconds ahead. Conner refused to allow himself to be drawn into a tacking duel. Bertrand threw twenty-seven tacks at the Americans but Conner, having gained this precious lead, now clamped a very firm cover on the Aussies, blocking every move they made. He played the shifts beautifully and at the same time covered the Australians. The wind was shifting from 5° to 10° and Conner was lucky with a few small wind shifts. He said later that boats only several hundred yards apart were in different sailing conditions with one on the inside of a lift going higher and looking faster. Steering through the steep, choppy seas was difficult.

Liberty rounded the second windward mark twenty-eight seconds ahead of *Australia II*. Her crew executed a perfect gybe-set heading downhill on the more favoured port gybe. Now it was Conner's turn to make what was, in retrospect, a serious mistake. He went left, thinking that the shifts would favour that side and make his course the shortest to the mark. It was also the side Conner calculated would be less influenced by spectator chop and the inevitable 'blanket' effect from so many boats blocking the breeze.

Australia II stayed on a much sharper angle to the mark and, for the third time that day, astonished the Americans with a blistering turn of downwind speed. She came round the mark with a bear-away set and went off to the right under a beautiful white spinnaker. She gybed two minutes later but that short starboard hitch put her in a better breeze. Within 400 metres of the leeward mark she had closed to within two and a half lengths of the Americans and 70 metres to the right of them. With the mark to the right of them both *Australia II* was nearer to it than *Liberty* and therefore almost on equal terms with the defender.

It was here that Conner and his crew executed one of the best and most daring moves of the entire summer. *Liberty*'s bowman, Scott Vogel, was sent forward to prepare for a lightning gybe. Surprise was absolutely vital, so Vogel slipped below and, unseen beneath the deck, went to the forehatch. When Conner gave the signal and swung the helm over, Vogel popped out like a jack-in-the-box and completed the dip-pole gybe in a flash. That left Bertrand with a couple of very quick decisions. Either he gybed with Conner or he crossed *Liberty*'s stern to try for an inside overlap at the mark. By gybing to starboard Conner threw the burden of keeping clear on to Bertrand. As the two boats converged on a collision course Bertrand put his helm hard down aiming, as he said later, to shoot across *Liberty's* stern and then gybe. It was a moment of tremendous stress for the steering gear. Suddenly there was a loud bang like a pistol shot as the rudder gear collapsed. One of five underdeck pulleys linking the rudder to the wheel ripped out of its welded bracket and sent *Australia II* into a wild broach. As the boat careered out of control her spinnaker pole went sky high and sent the great green-and-gold kite crashing and banging about overhead. Bertrand immediately grabbed the trim tab wheel, the device that controls the secondary rudder on the trailing edge of the keel. In the meantime tactician Hugh Treharne worked frantically to jury rig a block-and-tackle harness on the rudder. Bertrand did a wonderful job in regaining control through the trim tab but by this time they were almost at the mark with the spinnaker having to come down and the headsail go up. The kite went into the water and the headsail and main were not sheeted home for more than half a minute after the mark rounding. By that time *Liberty* had a comfortable lead of thirty-five seconds. The Australians sailed on for ten minutes, steering only with their trim tab while Treharne wedged himself in the cramped cavity aft to repair the damaged gear. The fact that *Australia II* managed to finish at all is a

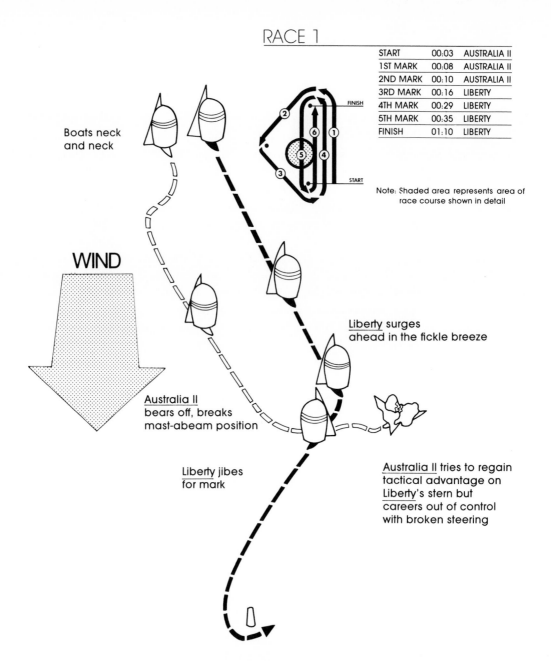

START	00:03	AUSTRALIA II
1ST MARK	00:08	AUSTRALIA II
2ND MARK	00:10	AUSTRALIA II
3RD MARK	00:16	LIBERTY
4TH MARK	00:29	LIBERTY
5TH MARK	00:35	LIBERTY
FINISH	01:10	LIBERTY

FINISH

START

Note: Shaded area represents area of race course shown in detail

Boats neck and neck

WIND

Liberty surges ahead in the fickle breeze

Australia II bears off, breaks mast-abeam position

Liberty jibes for mark

Australia II tries to regain tactical advantage on Liberty's stern but careers out of control with broken steering

RACE ONE

'Even though I had slight doubts about it, I considered the broken steering was strong enough. As it had been through hell and high water – and due to the pressure of building a new racing mast and the fact that every day had to be used to race or tune sails – it was overlooked. Murphy, true to his name, worked perfectly at the wrong time!' (Ben Lexcen) great tribute to his skill. *Liberty* won by 1 minute 10 seconds. This result was by no means a true indicator of the difference between the boats on the day. *Australia II* should have won and indeed she could have done so if her steering gear had not collapsed.

Ben felt personally responsible for the steering failure. 'I knew it was crook. . . . Steve Ward was forever nagging me for drawings of the steering system but I just didn't get round to it. Finally I agreed to his suggestion that he would simply make them like those he had worked on aboard the *Courageous*. When I first saw them I knew they weren't strong enough. I remember saying, "That's going to break," but it held together through several gales. We had the boat out in 50 knots once. And when it did break it wasn't blowing very hard. The sudden pressure was too much for it and it collapsed the weld.' Despite that first race loss Ben was convinced that *Australia II* was faster. 'We killed them on the first beat,' he said, and: 'We pulled them back a lot on the last beat. It was also clear that if the Americans mixed it up at the start they would be in trouble.'

Conner and his crew were given a hero's welcome when they sailed home to Newport. Thousands came down to her dock to cheer and whistle encouragement. The American boat was hauled out of the water. Conner was pleased but cautious: 'Wait until we've got three more on the board.'

Race Two
15 September
Liberty d. _Australia II_ by 1 minute 33 seconds

The second race also went to *Liberty*. A mechanical fault cost *Australia II* a victory. Six minutes before the start *Australia II* was gybing in a violent gust, estimated to be 24 knots true. She broke the uppermost of two specially hardened lugs used to secure the medium-air mainsail headboard to its carriage. The headboard swung down, pivoting around the lower lug, and then the whole head of the sail tore along the lower edge of the headboard. The mainsail leech, with nothing to support it but a 5-millimetre piece of Kevlar, sagged down a $\frac{1}{2}$ metre, giving the main all the grace and drive of an empty potato sack. After this disastrous beginning the *Australia II* crew not only went on with the race but very nearly won it, showing that she pointed higher and footed faster than the American defender.

The main boom was down at deck level but by raking the mast as far forward as it would go through hydraulic adjustment of the forestay the Australians were able to get a bit of tension back into the leech. While the breeze held steady at 17 knots they were able to sail very fast indeed. Dennis Conner recalled that realization as one of the most depressing parts of the entire cup campaign. Even though all the odds seemed stacked against them the Australians, through sheer sailing skill and a dogged, never-say-die attitude, were not to be easily defeated. The breeze was 030° at the start but as the race wore on it faded to 13 knots and fell into the east-north-east at 055°. That was disastrous for *Australia II*.

Liberty won the start by five seconds. *Australia II* was to windward at the gun but she tacked off soon after with *Liberty* going after her like a pathetic bird with a crippled wing. *Australia II*'s main flogged and thundered as she sailed off on a long port tack but she was first into a heading shift and not long after she tacked she crossed ahead of *Liberty*.

They split tacks again and when they came together seven minutes later *Australia II* was still in front. Conner initiated a savage tacking duel near the top mark in an attempt to aggravate *Australia II*'s mainsail problems but by this time the Australians had trimmed their rig so effectively that they survived eleven tacks in four minutes to hold *Liberty* out and carry her way past the starboard tack layline to the mark. It was an incredible comeback by the Australians. The 25° shift forced *Liberty* down into *Australia II*'s bad air. That meant the Americans were unable to lay the mark. Conner had to tack twice to clear it while the Australians scooted around forty-five seconds ahead and romped away under the by now familiar green-and-gold reaching kite. Bertrand was sailing a magnificent, faultless race.

Almost as soon as the spinnaker was up and drawing Colin Beashel went aloft in a bosun's chair. Beashel, a member of Sydney's legendary sailing Beashel clan, deserves special mention because his extraordinary natural skills kept Australian hopes alive. Working alone at the masthead, 28 metres above the water, he spent eighteen minutes on the two reaching legs, securing the head of the main to the masthead carriage with lashing rove through a hole he punched with a spike. *Liberty* narrowed the gap to thirty-one seconds at the gybe mark and thirty-one seconds at the leeward mark. Despite Beashel's skill the Australians could not haul the main up to its full height.

The easing breeze meant an end to Australian hopes as *Liberty* relentlessly pulled them back on the fourth leg. Conner caught them halfway up that 4.5-mile leg. Towards the end of the leg the protest incident occurred when Conner dropped what the Americans call a 'slam-dunk' manoeuvre on the Australians. As he crossed he tacked immediately and upwind to bring the Australians directly under his wind shadow. *Australia II* immediately hoisted a red protest flag. Bertrand alleged that the American tactic had forced him to alter course to avoid collision.

The five-man international jury took the entire day following to discuss the incident and eventually disallowed the protest. They maintained that *Australia II* could have missed *Liberty* if Bertrand had held his course. The jury gave the following reason for their decision: '*Australia II* could have kept clear of *Liberty* either by maintaining course or by tacking as she did to avoid *Liberty*'s covering

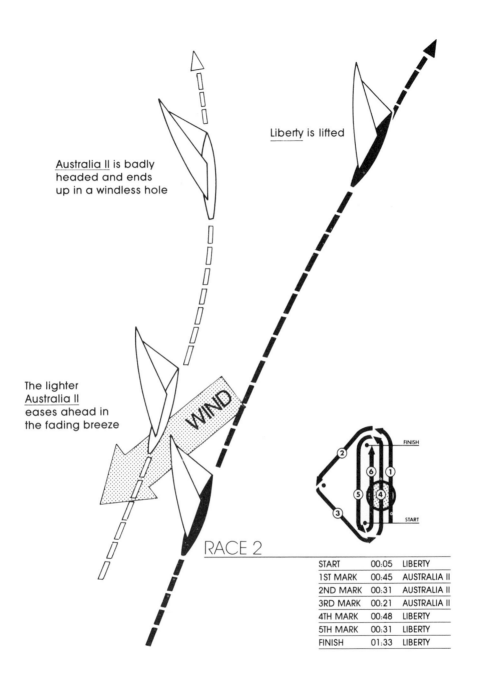

Liberty is lifted

Australia II is badly headed and ends up in a windless hole

The lighter Australia II eases ahead in the fading breeze

WIND

RACE 2

START	00:05	LIBERTY
1ST MARK	00:45	AUSTRALIA II
2ND MARK	00:31	AUSTRALIA II
3RD MARK	00:21	AUSTRALIA II
4TH MARK	00:48	LIBERTY
5TH MARK	00:31	LIBERTY
FINISH	01:33	LIBERTY

RACE TWO
'Luck of the game, and *Australia II* was crippled with a broken headboard.' (Ben Lexcen)

tack. *Liberty* has satisfied the jury that she completed her tack in accordance with rule 41.' Alan Bond was clearly disappointed with the decision. He said that *Australia II*'s bowman, Damian Fewster, had testified that the gap between the two boats was more like 24 inches. Bond said he would study the results and see what 'appropriate action' could be taken. 'We are not saying that the jury came to a decision which was wrong,' he told a press conference, 'but we are saying that the evidence admitted was biased.' Bond was convinced that the jury should have given more weight to Fewster's on-the-spot observation rather than the videotape shot taken from the hovering blimp.

Liberty came around the fourth mark forty-eight seconds in front and *Australia II* was never able to get close to her again. The Australians did stage a comeback of sorts when they pulled them back to thirty-one seconds after the downhill run under spinnakers but on the final beat to the finish their crippled state became more and more obvious in the light air. The breeze had swung 25° and the new course was signalled by the Race Committee boat *Black Knight*. As the breeze faded it backed and veered in a series of 20° shifts. In those circumstances Bertrand and Treharne felt they had nothing to lose by going off in search of a breeze. They split tacks in a last, bold gamble that they might dig into a wind shift to the left. They never found it and *Liberty* came home an easy winner by 1 minute 30 seconds.

The race was over but the arguing continued. There was a dispute over a call for a lay day. Each side claimed that the other had called for it first but the New York Yacht Club Race Committee decided that the Australians had asked for the lay day. While the Australian afterguard argued, the rest of the crew spent the entire day overhauling every piece of equipment.

With the score now 2–0 the Australians faced the grim prospect of going the way of every other challenger ever to contest for the cup. 'We were two down and looking down the barrel,' said Ben, 'and the public perception was, "Oh well, there go the Aussies again, getting the shit kicked out of them."' Ben started to come to terms with the possibility of defeat. 'From that day on I resigned myself to the fact that maybe we wouldn't get through. And I knew that if we didn't beat them this time, then there was simply no point trying any more. This was our best shot.' Warren Jones was uncharacteristically grim-faced in his dockside office as he commented: 'We've got to win this next one or we're done for. It's bad enough being 2–0 but coming back from 3–0 would be beyond even Lazarus.' This was a side of Jones that the *Australia II* crew rarely, if ever, saw. So far as the crew were concerned they would win the cup. After all Jones had already chalked the victory into his planning board. The space under 24 September, his birthday, said 'Win the cup'. He was only two days out.

Race Three
17 September (abandoned)
Rerun 18 September
Australia II d. *Liberty* **by 3 minutes 14 seconds**

On Saturday, 17 September over 1,500 boats turned out to see whether Australia could put a win on the board. She did, but the clock beat her. This unfinished race showed beyond doubt the fact that *Australia II* was vastly superior to *Liberty* in light air. *Australia II* became the first challenger in 113 years of cup competition to lead the American defender around every mark of the course. She could have won against *Liberty* had the time limit of 5 hours 15 minutes not run out as she raced within sight of the finish.

Australia II sailed so well that *Liberty* looked completely outclassed. The race started in a perfect 10-knot south-south-easterly and Bertrand, having won the start in a decisive fashion, went on to round the first mark ahead for the third successive time, leading Liberty by 1 minute 15 seconds. The heavier *Liberty* was simply no match for the Australian boat and at the end of the two reaching legs she was 1 minute 58 seconds astern.

Liberty's skipper, Dennis Conner, realized he had no means of defence against the Australian boat's obvious turning superiority, and indeed her all-round superiority in the light air. It was blowing 8 knots from the south-south-east as Conner elected to run away from the line and down towards the base of a great arc of spectator boats, away to leeward of the start.

Australia II's phenomenal turning ability, the ability to spin like a top and still keep going, meant that the American skipper had to forget about any attempt to fight for the most favoured right-hand side of the line and go instead for a timed start, aiming to hit the line at speed on the gun. It did not work on either account. Bertrand had no trouble in starting well to windward, eleven seconds ahead of *Liberty*. That was the beginning of the end for the Americans. *Australia II* romped away in the light air. Ten minutes after the gun *Liberty* tacked to port and tried to sneak over to the new breeze which Bertrand was enjoying on the right. When *Australia II* tacked to cover her the awesome extent of her advantage became obvious. Bertrand had opened out a clear five boat lengths on *Liberty*. Having won the right-hand side of the course Bertrand maintained a solid, blocking defence, making absolutely sure that *Liberty* was severely punished with dirty air every time she tried to zip across to the better breeze.

Conner initiated a tacking duel in slow motion, only to find that with each and every tack he threw at them, The Australians went further and further ahead. The Australian boat not only tacked more easily, it also accelerated out of the tacks faster.

A quarter of a mile before the first mark *Liberty* changed to a lighter headsail and *Australia II* immediately followed suit. By this time the breeze was down to no more than 6 knots. What had started out as a grey, miserable and threatening day turned into a fearfully hot and airless one. There were twenty-one tacks on the first leg, with shifts from 30° to 45°. These shifts were so significant that, at one stage, when *Australia II* looked certain to have to make two quick final tacks around the windward mark, she was in fact able to lift up almost miraculously and lay it in one. That put *Australia II* ahead by 1 minute 15 seconds at the top mark. The first leg had taken fifty-two minutes to sail and while that seemed to many an agonizingly long time to sail 4.5 miles, much worse was to come.

Australia II set one of the spinnakers she had borrowed from the failed Melbourne boat, *Challenge 12*. It was a lovely little flat-cut spinnaker, red, white and blue and ideally suited to the light conditions. *Liberty* came up with her familiar red, white and blue kite but it was nowhere near as effective.

The top third of the leech on *Liberty*'s mainsail seemed to be ineffective in the light air and it kept curling in and collapsing as she made her way down what had become an almost square run because of the 45° shift. Both boats gybed five times down the first spinnaker leg with *Australia II* pulling away steadily with each change of course. The Australians rounded the wing mark two minutes ahead of *Liberty* and immediately doused their spinnaker and went instead for a light headsail. *Liberty* also dropped her kite but then set an all-Mylar gennaker, a cross between a flat-reaching spinnaker and a genoa. This did her no good at all.

Towards the end of this leg *Black Knight* came steaming up the course signalling the changed direction of the second windward mark. It was 215° or south-south-west. That meant there had been a shift of 60° while the boats raced round the triangle.

Australia II rounded the leeward mark 1 minute 58 seconds ahead of *Liberty*. Eleven minutes after the rounding *Liberty* changed to a lighter, all-Mylar headsail. By this time the breeze had dropped to no more than 5 knots. *Australia II* followed suit with a lighter headsail of her own but this one had khaki-coloured Kevlar panels reinforcing its leech. Towards the top of the second windward leg, *Liberty* sailed on port to the very fringes of the vast spectator fleet in pursuit of a new breeze from the right. Bertrand, conscious of time running out, elected to break off the close cover he had maintained throughout the race and instead go direct for the windward mark. That was his one mistake in an otherwise faultless race. The moment he let Conner off the hook *Liberty* started to improve. Immediately Bertrand realized his mistake he tacked back to cover.

Australia II made sixteen tacks on this second windward leg to *Liberty*'s thirteen. The Australians rounded the mark 1 minute 46 seconds ahead. Once again *Australia II* set the same beautifully effective red, white and blue spinnaker. At this stage there were only 2 hours and 6 minutes to finish the race and already anxious Australian faces glanced at their watches. On *Australia II*'s tender, *Black Swan*, Ben Lexcen got down on his hands and knees in mock prayer while her backup helmsman, Sir James Hardy, signalled across the water that maybe a pair of oars was needed.

The race had to be completed within the statutory time limit of 5 hours 15 minutes. It was not impossible but with each passing moment in the light and listless air, it looked more and more unlikely that *Australia II* would beat the clock. Two-thirds of the way down the fifth leg both boats fell into a huge windless hole. *Australia II* eventually managed to pick up a slant and ghosted to a leeward mark which she rounded an astonishing 5 minutes 57 seconds ahead of *Liberty*. This was the largest single gap any cup challenger had ever opened up over an American defender.

At this stage *Australia II* had just sixty-two minutes left to sail the last 4.5-mile leg to the finish. The Australians were so desperate that they even put one of their crew men, Skip Lossiman, up the mast as far as the hounds to scout for a breeze. With just twenty-five minutes left *Australia II* ignored the match race she was in and went looking for her own breeze off to the right. She found it but too late. Time ran out with the breeze filling in beautifully but *Australia II* still about fifteen minutes shy of the line. John Bertrand said later that it was about three minutes before this that his navigator, Grant Simmer, calculated that they would have to sail the last leg at an average of 30 knots to win. *Australia II* was fast but not quite that fast. With 1½ miles to the line the Race Committee raised the dreaded 'A' flag to signal race abandoned. The score remained 2–0 in the defender's favour.

After one and a half hours' delay the third race rematch got under way at 1.40 p.m. on Sunday, 18 September in a true south-westerly wind, 225° of 7 knots. This was to be *Australia II*'s day. From the outset *Australia II* was so completely *Liberty*'s mistress in the light stuff that it was a question not of whether she would win but by how much. No one, not even the eternally ebullient Alan Bond, could have predicted so devastating a walkover as 3 minutes 14 seconds.

These were, once again, perfect conditions for *Australia II* and Conner seemed reluctant to tangle with Bertrand in the pre-start manoeuvres. Conner left Bertrand alone and went for the Committee Boat end of the line. The Australian weathermen correctly predicted that the left-hand side of the track would be favoured early in the race as the young south-west breeze filled in, matured and then followed the traditional swing to the right. Conner wanted the right-hand side of the south-south-westerly and the Australians were more than delighted to give it to him. Although *Liberty* is credited with an eight-second advantage at the gun the gap between the two boats was in fact even greater. *Australia II* was moving much faster than the defender because Conner had to luff almost head-to-wind to clear the long anchor line set by the committee.

Both boats set off fairly evenly on port with *Australia II* to leeward by about four boat lengths. The early part of the first leg soon became a test of pure straight-line speed, a 'drag race' as the Americans called it. Both boats stood-on on port tack for twenty-two minutes in this extraordinary test of sheer speed. *Australia II* had the edge, sailing a steady 2° higher and steadily climbing out to windward.

Twenty-two minutes after the gun, when *Liberty* eventually tacked on to starboard, *Australia II* crossed ahead with an advantage of five boat lengths. Conner tossed seven tacks at the Australians to try to break free of their covering grip but *Australia II* was easily able to stay in control by virtue of her speed through tacks and her ability to accelerate quickly out of them. It was as if *Australia II* had some secret power source and of course this is precisely what the winged keel was. At the first mark she was 1 minute 40 seconds ahead. The Australian crew work was superb.

Liberty closed to within fifty-two seconds at the wing mark and, capitalizing on a tighter second reaching leg in which she made very good use of a transparent Mylar staysail, she gained a further ten seconds. By this time, however, *Liberty* was already too far behind to pose any serious threat.

That forty-two-second edge at the leeward mark enabled the Australians to clamp a very effective cover on the Americans. There was a real sense of desperation about the American tactic on the second windward leg. Conner tried everything: straight-line sailing for speed, quick tacking, headsail changes, but nothing seemed to make the slightest impression on the Australian flying machine. Whenever *Liberty* tacked her crew had to ease her headsail while Conner bore off a point or two to power up and get the boat moving again. *Australia II* by contrast just flipped about and accelerated away. In the 12-knot breeze she was averaging 7 knots. During a tack this fell sometimes as little as half a knot, but within fifteen seconds it was back up to 7 knots again. This was the kind of speed *Liberty* had to contend with.

Australia II went away to a lead of 1 minute 15 seconds at the end of the fourth leg and stretched that to 2 minutes 47 seconds at the end of the square run. With the memory of the cancelled race still fresh in their minds *Australia II*'s hierarchy aboard the *Black Swan* were casting the odd anxious glance at their watches, but they need not have worried. On the last leg *Australia II* showed tremendous power and pointing ability in the 10-knot breeze to win by 3 minutes 14 seconds.

The great American boat, *Liberty*, had been made to look ordinary and the previously unbeatable Conner was now revealed as an ordinary mortal. It was only the ninth win by a challenger in 103 years and the history books revealed it as the second biggest win by a challenger since *Livonia* beat *Columbia* by 5 minutes 10 seconds over a 35-mile course off New York in 1870.

Newport went wild at the news of the Australian win. There were an estimated 5,000 Australians in town and every one of them seemed to be down at the

RACE 3

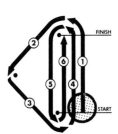

START	00:08	LIBERTY
1ST MARK	01:14	AUSTRALIA II
2ND MARK	00:52	AUSTRALIA II
3RD MARK	00:42	AUSTRALIA II
4TH MARK	01:15	AUSTRALIA II
5TH MARK	02:47	AUSTRALIA II
FINISH	03:14	AUSTRALIA II

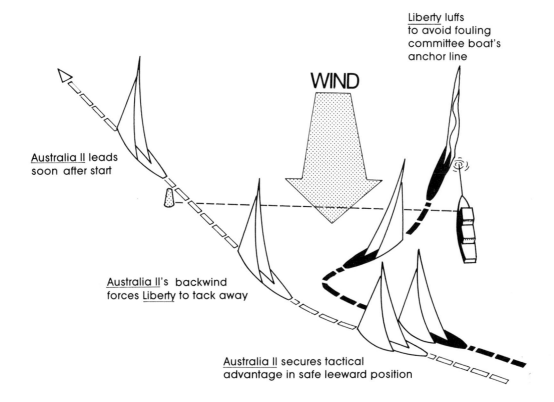

Liberty luffs
to avoid fouling
committee boat's
anchor line

WIND

Australia II leads
soon after start

Australia II's backwind
forces Liberty to tack away

Australia II secures tactical
advantage in safe leeward position

RACE THREE

'*Australia II* forced *Liberty* to tack and go to the wrong end of the starting line. *Liberty* should have tacked rather than luff around the starting boat, although this is a hindsight observation. Actually, Dennis Conner did the right thing in trying to port tack out first, and fortunately the wind went *Australia II*'s way.' (Ben Lexcen)

Australia II dock when she came home in the gathering darkness, surrounded by a great flotilla of small craft. One rubber boat was crewed by a man in a kangaroo costume and someone else turned up dressed as a giant koala. There were sirens, whistles, horns and cheers as the crew hauled the boat up and carted their sails ashore. The Australians had won a race, but it seemed as if they had taken the cup itself.

Australia II still shrouded after winning Race Three

Dennis Conner called for a lay day on 19 September. *Liberty* clearly needed a real breeze to match the Australians. Gary Jobson, tactician aboard the American defence contender, *Defender*, who covered the series with me for ABC, gave his old rival Conner full marks for trying. 'Conner and his crew did everything perfectly,' he said. 'They tried to draw Bertrand into mistakes in tacking duels, they tried to attack him on the reaches, and they gybed seven times to what could have been favourable wind slants on the run. They were just outclassed by boat speed. In the conditions today *Australia II* is truly a "Superboat".'

The Australians used the time off to check every item of gear and to replace their slightly buckled forestay. They were leaving nothing to chance for what would be the most decisive race of the series.

Race Four
20 September
Liberty d. *Australia II* by 43 seconds

Race Four started in magnificent conditions, typical of Newport in the late summer. The breeze was west-south-west 235° and at 10 knots for the start. *Liberty* won the start by six seconds, and with it the race. Australia lost the fourth race through a simple six-second miscalculation which put her in the extraordinary position of then having to win three races in a row.

In the early stages of the pre-start manoeuvres Bertrand kept Conner bobbing and weaving, both men wanting to secure the favoured right-hand side of the line, the side from which the 12-knot south-westerly wind would phase. With a minute to go Bertrand seemed to misjudge his position in relation to the line. He had planned to cross on starboard tack near its right-hand end, timing his approach so that Conner, who was on port, would have to dip behind to observe the right-of-way, port–starboard rule. *Australia II* was sitting in a stalled head-to-head situation with *Liberty*, with just three and a half minutes left, when she broke off and appeared to sail too far away from the line to duck back in time. With about sixty seconds to the gun *Australia II* was on starboard and close to the committee boat end of the line, while *Liberty* on port tack headed for the committee boat. Conner showed the judgmental skill and icy calm that had made him a legendary figure in international yachting when he held his course and crossed no more than 10 or perhaps 15 feet in front of *Australia II* to win the start by six seconds. Bertrand conceded later that he misjudged the start: 'It was,' he said, 'purely a judgmental error on my part.' *Liberty* stood to the right of the upwind leg for three minutes, deliberately ignoring *Australia II*'s uncovered tack course to the left. With the practised eye of the world's most experienced 12-metre skipper Conner picked the shifts. One shift on the right soon after the start lifted him up 6°. Another on the left lifted him 16°. The Americans knew what they were doing and never looked back. The defender got all the lifts that traditionally favour the right-hand track in a south-westerly wind while the Australians, who stuck resolutely to the left, got all the knocks.

In the moderate air and a relatively flat sea the two boats were fairly evenly matched. It came down to a matter of who picked the shifts first. Conner went to the boat's speed and in doing so seemed to show complete disregard for conventional match race wisdom. Faced with a boat he knew he could not out-tack he scarcely even bothered to tack to cover. *Australia II* made only six tacks on this first windward leg, *Liberty* made five. It became another 'drag race', a contest of pure speed. When they came together *Liberty* had shot into a commanding lead. At the first mark the Americans were thirty-six seconds ahead.

Liberty gained twelve seconds on the first reaching leg and the margin remained forty-eight seconds at the leeward mark. Conner and Whidden ignored the traditional match race tactics that demanded that a leading boat stay between its opponent and the mark and went instead in search of every slant they could find. The Australians were left with no option other than to follow on. They did, and *Liberty* led them round the second windward mark by forty-six seconds.

RACE 4

START	00:06	LIBERTY
1ST MARK	00:36	LIBERTY
2ND MARK	00:48	LIBERTY
3RD MARK	00:48	LIBERTY
4TH MARK	00:46	LIBERTY
5TH MARK	00:35	LIBERTY
FINISH	00:43	LIBERTY

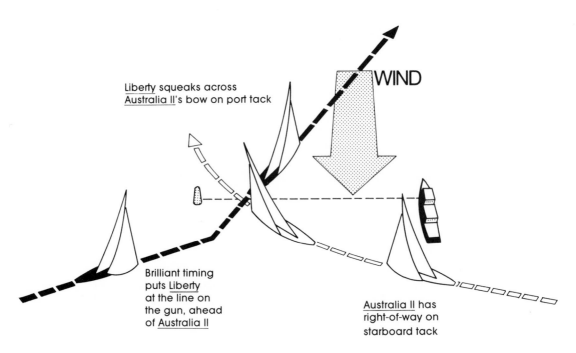

Liberty squeaks across Australia II's bow on port tack

WIND

Brilliant timing puts <u>Liberty</u> at the line on the gun, ahead of <u>Australia II</u>

Australia II has right-of-way on starboard tack

RACE FOUR
'This was bad judgement on the part of Dennis Conner but *Liberty* went on to win the most superb sail race I have ever seen.' (Ben Lexcen)

Australia II returns to Newport

Australia II had already established a reputation as a downhill flyer but she was too far behind in these conditions to do anything more than take eleven seconds out of the Americans. She rounded thirty-five seconds astern but with the breeze freshening to 15 knots for the final beat and the Americans capitalizing on every wind shift, *Liberty* was able to walk away to a comfortable forty-three-second win.

Both boats were enveloped in a great mob of spectator craft after the finish. The air was rent with the sound of sirens, whistles, horns and cheers as the Americans swept home to Newport in triumph. There was no lesser welcome for the Australians. Once again the fans aboard the 1,000-odd spectator boats had been treated to a magnificent display of close match racing.

When someone asked Alan Bond what it felt like to be 3–1 down, Bondy, in typical feisty fashion, said he felt just like an Anzac at Gallipoli. 'We had our backs to the wall there,' he said 'and we won that one.' It took another Australian to remind him that the tragedy at Anzac Cove was in truth one of the worst military disasters in the history of modern warfare and that in the end the original 'Diggers' had to be taken off that bloody Turkish beach-head by British boats. The defiant Bondy said that what he meant by the Anzac analogy was that Australians do not give up without a fight. Indeed, the race on the following day, 21 September would be a do-or-die effort. Alan Bond said once again, very firmly, that whichever way it went, it would certainly be his last America's Cup campaign. He was convinced that if he could not win the America's Cup after a campaign as intensive as this one had been then no one could.

As *Australia II* backed up into her berth at Newport Offshore a weary John Bertrand looked up and said to me: 'I'll never endure a humiliation like that again.' Bertrand was as good as his word.

Race Five
21 September
Australia II d. *Liberty* by 1 minute 47 seconds

After so many faults had emerged to plague the Australians, it seemed only fair to many of their supporters that the Americans should have their share as well. An hour before the fifth race started, while *Liberty* was tuning up with her trial horse, *Freedom*, she bent the ¾-inch-diameter stainless-steel hydraulic ram which tensions the aluminium jumper struts. The struts collapsed and with them went effective control of the upper third of the American mast and, through it, control of the upper part of the powerful mainsail.

Liberty at first sought permission from the Race Committee to have a spare strut flown out by helicopter. When this request was turned down, it sent its fastest support boat, the 40-knot skiff *Rhonda*, dashing back the 11 miles to Castle Hill at the entrance to Narragansett Bay where it picked up the spare jumpers from an inflatable runabout.

In the meantime, *Liberty*'s bowman, Scott Vogel, and Tom Rich, her pitman, were sent aloft to dismantle the collapsed jumpers. Vogel and Rich deserve the highest praise for an extraordinary display of great courage and seamanship. They stayed aloft and worked on the swaying mast despite a nasty, lumpy sea that pitched them about, leaving them badly bruised. The replacement was passed to *Liberty* and the work completed just two minutes before the ten-minute warning gun sounded. Vogel and Rich had spent fifty minutes up the mast and they returned to the deck exhausted and clearly in no condition to race. None the less they did. As part of the three-man foredeck gang they had to get on immediately with the task of setting the headsail as the yachts prepared to come together for the vital pre-start manoeuvres. Conner paid special tribute to Rich and Vogel. 'I don't know many men,' he said, 'who could have endured that sort of punishment at the top of a mast for so long.' With a breeze which was west-south-westerly, 190° and in a lumpy, confused sea, the American defender, if not crippled as Dennis Conner claimed, was certainly handicapped. Rich, in his haste to make up for lost time, had accidentally ripped the luff tapes on *Liberty*'s best heavy-weather jib. *Australia II* was already coming at them down the line when *Liberty* was forced to run away from her bare-headed.

Australia leapt to attack the disadvantaged Americans but Conner soon threw them off by wheeling around behind an enormous coastguard ship. Bertrand and his afterguard misjudged the start by something under a metre and although they had pushed *Liberty* over the line early, the Americans were able to duck back and successfully recross while the Australians sat almost motionless in the water on the wrong side of the line. *Liberty* was off and running on port tack while *Australia II* was forced to ease away, run back behind the line, gybe and set out in pursuit fully thirty seconds astern. All Australian hearts sank at that moment when it looked as if the entire cup summer was suddenly over. It was by far the worst start of the entire series and it demonstrated clearly just how fine a line there is between a brilliant manoeuvre and one that brings forth the scorn of all the armchair admirals.

Three or four minutes after the start *Liberty*'s port jumper strut gave way again. The repair work had not been completely effective because the hydraulic cylinder had been damaged and the steel rod remained fully extended. Without proper tension on the jumpers *Liberty*'s mast sagged off badly whenever she sailed off port tack. *Liberty* was sailing as fast as *Australia II* but lower on port. It was a severe handicap and yet Conner held on to port tack because he expected that the shifts would clock right. They did not. *Australia II* tacked away from *Liberty* on to starboard and made the middle of the course. Conner stayed on port for five minutes before he realized the gravity of his error. *Australia II* sailed into a 5° header and when she tacked back the Americans lost their lead of three and a half boat lengths. As they came together again twenty-seven minutes after the start they were dead even. 'When I saw Dennis was not going to cover us, my heart leapt,' Bertrand said later. 'I figured, this is an opportunity we are going to take with a vengeance. All of a sudden we were right in the money.' For a while they raced neck and neck, no more than a few feet apart. Eventually Conner was forced to tack away when *Australia II* began to draw ahead.

After ten very quick tacks in just five minutes *Australia II* had regained her lead. There was no 12-metre yacht in the world that could tack and accelerate as quickly as *Australia II*. The Australians timed their tacks to dump the maximum amount of dirty or disturbed air on the American sails whenever they caught *Liberty* on starboard tack. They gave her free air on port tack and thereby encouraged Conner to go right. At all costs the Australians wanted to protect their advantage on the left.

Australia II made twenty-one tacks on this first windward leg to *Liberty*'s twenty. At the windward mark *Australia II* seemed certain to have to make two extra hitches to round the mark but in an exceptionally daring piece of sailing, Bertrand shot *Australia II*, with its huge main and genoa shivering in the breeze, high into the eye of the wind and skated around the buoy. Conner did the same. *Australia II* rounded the top mark twenty-three seconds ahead and held precisely the same margin at the wing mark. She had taken only forty-six minutes to sail that first

RACE 5

START	00:37	LIBERTY
1ST MARK	00:23	AUSTRALIA II
2ND MARK	00:23	AUSTRALIA II
3RD MARK	00:18	AUSTRALIA II
4TH MARK	01:11	AUSTRALIA II
5TH MARK	00:52	AUSTRALIA II
FINISH	01:47	AUSTRALIA II

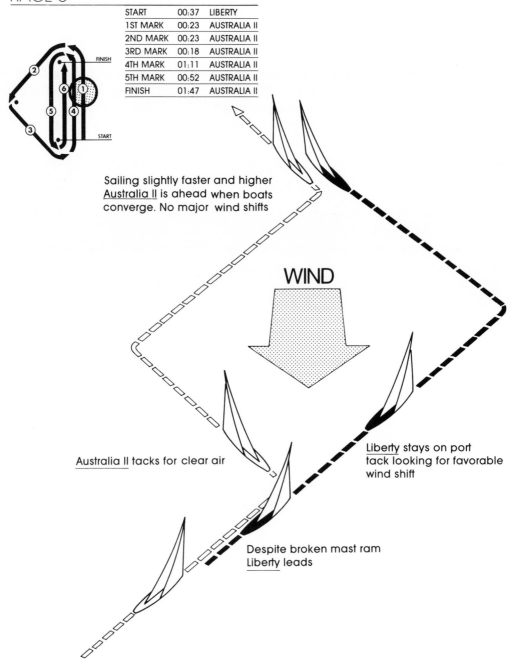

Sailing slightly faster and higher
Australia II is ahead when boats
converge. No major wind shifts

WIND

Australia II tacks for clear air

Liberty stays on port
tack looking for favorable
wind shift

Despite broken mast ram
Liberty leads

RACE FIVE
'*Liberty* was probably slowed down by a broken mast ram.' (Ben Lexcen)

4.5-mile leg. It was by far the fastest time recorded for any windward leg in this America's Cup series. *Liberty* pegged them back to eighteen seconds by the leeward mark. On this vital second windward leg it became obvious that *Liberty*'s port jumper was worse than useless. It had collapsed completely allowing the top third of the mast to sag off to leeward whenever the boat was heeled on a port tack. This distorted the smooth driving aerofoil shape of the main and although Dennis Conner was later reluctant to suggest what this might have cost him in terms of time, he did concede that it had placed a very severe psychological burden on him. The wind howled in at 21 knots on the second beat and the Race Committee boat, *Black Knight*, signalled a 10° course change to 185°, just west of south. Australia shot ahead, pointing higher and accelerating much faster out of tacks, to round the fourth mark a very comfortable 1 minute 11 seconds ahead.

The Americans set a very big spinnaker for the square run which helped them pull the Australians back fifty-two seconds at the bottom mark. That margin was more than enough for *Australia II* and with Bertrand applying only a loose cover they raced away to a very convincing 1 minute 47 seconds' win.

It was the first time a 12-metre challenger had ever won two races in a cup series. *Gretel II* had, of course, won two races but had subsequently been disqualified by what was then the NYYC's protest committee in 1970. *Australia II* was surrounded by a wildly cheering mob of spectators after the gun and they stayed with her in an escort flotilla all the way back to Newport Harbour. There, under an enormous Australian flag, fully 45 × 20 feet, she was clapped and cheered back into her green canvas security shield. The score now stood at 3–2. Bertrand had at least had the satisfaction of erasing some of the race humiliation he had spoken so passionately about previously. It was a great win for *Australia II* but still a do-or-die struggle. The sixth race would tell whether the Australians were about to write another chapter in the history books, as the first boat to go 3–3, or whether she would simply join the long list of challengers who had bravely tried but failed to win the America's Cup.

Race Six
22 September
Australia II **d.** *Liberty* **by 3 minutes 25 seconds**

Thursday, 22 September was a historic day both for *Australia II* and for the America's Cup competition. It was the day when she became the first challenger in the 113-year history of the event to square a match 3–all and her winning margin of 3 minutes 25 seconds was the largest ever recorded by a 12-metre challenger.

Both challenger and defender bristled with electronic devices that could tell them precisely where they were, how well they were sailing, how far to the layline, what the breeze was doing and a lot more. In the vital sixth race, however, it seemed that all those expensive instruments counted for nothing. The race would be decided on the first windward leg when, in the fickle, shifting, north-north-westerly wind, Australian tactician Hugh Treharne and skipper John Bertrand looked across the water, as any small-boat sailor might do, and saw the dark line of a monumental wind shift bearing down upon them from the left. Dennis Conner admitted candidly after the race that he and the men aboard *Liberty* did not see it. The laconic Bertrand needed all his powers of understatement to conceal his sheer joy at outsmarting his old rival: 'Yes, we were surprised, but Dennis was obviously playing the wind shifts as we were and he figured, I assume, they were going to the right. We were happy to be going to the left from the signs we could see on the water.'

The boats were so evenly matched that once again the results would depend not so much on sailing brilliance as on simple, unforgivable mistakes. Conner made his and paid for it, but not before Bertrand stopped all Australian hearts with yet another of his mistimed starts.

The wind was a cool 12-knot north-north-westerly, 340°, that would later back to the west, forcing two course changes for the second and final beats, and freshen to between 16 and 19 knots. Bertrand misjudged his start for the third successive race. After approaching it too early on starboard tack he had to gybe, circle and cross behind *Liberty* on port, recrossing seven seconds late at the line. *Liberty* tacked to port and was nicely placed on the inside of a lift that helped her cross *Australia II* which came back on starboard. The Australians stayed on starboard and went way off to the left-hand side of the course. The Americans followed them four minutes after the start.

After fourteen minutes *Australia II* tacked on to port. Conner tacked in front of them and ahead by two boat lengths. That forced the Australians to tack away and into a header. Conner was content to hang on to his port tack lift ignoring *Australia II*. When Bertrand tacked back on to port he found himself on *Liberty*'s quarter.

Now it was the Australians' turn to benefit from the patchy breeze. While *Liberty* sailed into a lull and was forced to bear away, *Australia II* found herself in a fresher patch and began to lift out and up in a dramatic comeback. After ten minutes *Liberty* sailed into a light header, tacked to starboard and staggered back towards the Australians.

Australia II came back at *Liberty* and dumped so much dirty air on the Americans that Conner was forced to tack away back on to port. That manoeuvre put *Australia II* into an extraordinary port tack lift. She tacked into it and lifted almost straight to the windward mark. *Liberty* was left a long way to leeward in very much lighter air. The breeze dropped to no more than 5 knots at the mark and

RACE 6

START	00:07	LIBERTY
1ST MARK	02:29	AUSTRALIA II
2ND MARK	02:48	AUSTRALIA II
3RD MARK	03:46	AUSTRALIA II
4TH MARK	03:22	AUSTRALIA II
5TH MARK	04:08	AUSTRALIA II
FINISH	03:25	AUSTRALIA II

Australia II gets
strong 15° lift,
to take lead

WIND

Australia II forced to short tack away from
Liberty's backwind

RACE SIX
'Once again, Dennis Conner had to gamble because of the limited ability of *Liberty*. The
Australia II crew benefited from this gambling.' (Ben Lexcen)

Australia II came round with a huge lead of 2 minutes 29 seconds. Dennis Conner had committed his second major match mistake in two races. It is, of course, easy to be wise after the event, but it is difficult to accept Conner's explanation that he simply did not see the wind shift. Conner was believed to have had *Freedom*, his trial horse, out there to windward acting as an enormous wind-vein, a sort of telltale that should have been signalling the shift. If the Americans had been looking they would have seen *Freedom* lifting up on the same shift that won the lead for *Australia II.*

The Australians lost only one second on the first reach as they swept around the wing mark with a beautifully executed gybe in which they simultaneously peeled to a running spinnaker for the third leg which had become a run. She came round the bottom mark 3 minutes 46 seconds ahead. The Race Committee signalled a course change to 295° for the second windward leg but the breeze continued to freshen and swing into the south-west. *Australia II* clamped an extremely effective cover on *Liberty* all the way up the second beat, blocking any prospect for recovery she may have had. She rounded 3 minutes 22 seconds ahead and was now so far in front that it was not a question of whether she would win but by how much.

The American yacht seemed to be labouring under an enormous psychological burden and one could understand why. No other defender had come this close to losing the precious cup. Conner knew that the old cliché about his head replacing the cup was not so much a joke as a promise as far as certain NYYC blackcoats were concerned. It was an indication of just how desperate and frustrated Conner had become when he quite deliberately came at *Australia II* close-hauled on starboard tack as they came down the fifth leg under spinnaker. It was all quite within the racing rules: a boat on the free leg of the course – *Australia II* – must give way to a boat close-hauled – *Liberty*. There were those, however, including Alan Bond, who found it grossly unfair that the American had set out to force a foul which could have disqualified *Australia II.* Bond was less than impressed by what he clearly felt was a dirty trick: 'There are some things you do in yachting, and some things you do not do. This was one thing you definitely do not do.'

Bertrand, however, saw what was happening and hardened up so that he cleared *Liberty*'s bow by two boat lengths. When Conner realized his foul was not going to work he tacked to port and went for the buoy. 'The only chance we had to beat them was to foul them out,' said Tom Whidden, *Liberty*'s tactician. 'I have a feeling they thought that was illegal but it's not, as long as you don't alter course to seek them out. There is a rule against that.' *Australia II* came round the leeward mark by the biggest margin any challenger had ever established over a cup defender. She was 4 minutes 8 seconds ahead of *Liberty* and covered easily on the last leg to finish the race 3 minutes 25 seconds in front.

The gun from the committee boat signalled a tremendous wave of support for

Australia II. Americans in their thousands came to stand twelve deep around the *Australia II* dock, to cheer, stamp and whistle their hope that at long last, after twenty-one years of trying, the Australians might be on the brink of beating the NYYC.

Alan Bond surprised everyone an hour later when the Australians flew their blue-and-white-chequered November flag signalling that they did not want to race the following day. Bond's public explanation was that he wanted the crew to rest and have the boat checked over thoroughly. The reality, however, was that the Australians were well aware that the forecast for the following day indicated the kind of variable wind which could have turned this climactic race into a lottery. The Australians also realized that any delay at this late stage would put even greater psychological pressure on Dennis Conner and the American crew men.

Security at the *Australia II* dock was redoubled after the sixth race win. The regular armed guard detail was strengthened by a dozen Australian volunteers who took turns protecting the challenger around the clock. The Australians were not taking any chances now that they were so close to winning the cup. Concern about security in Newport increased when two of the Australian two-way radios were stolen after the yacht had returned to her berth. The radios, used for communication between the racing yacht and her tender, were valued at close on $1,000. It was not the value that disturbed the Australians, however, but the realization that someone with less than honest intentions had come so close to their multi-million-dollar racing machine. Alan Bond also revealed that a diver had been spotted in the water near the entrance to the *Australia II* dock at two o'clock on the morning of the sixth race. Security men had seen the diver surface several hundred yards away and then disappear into the early morning gloom. According to Bond a check of the Australian dock revealed that a rope with plastic rubbish bags attached to it had been found strung across the entrance to the berth. If undiscovered, it would have snared the winged keel and acted as a sea anchor, slowing the boat to a snail's pace.

These were some of the elements that contributed to a rising tide of Australian paranoia. They feared that having come so far their final bid for the cup might somehow be denied them. In the event nothing happened. By now all of sport-mad Australia was awake to the very real possibility that, after twenty years of defeat, a gang of Australian yachtsmen were now about to win the supreme prize of prizes. In a nation where all sport is followed with a fervour akin to religious devotion, millions of people who had never heard of Rhode Island Sound, let alone seen a 12-metre yacht, were suddenly victims of America's Cup fever. The entire country was hooked, listening to every minute detail of a race that had once been described with derision as being as exciting as watching grass grow or paint dry. Race Seven, which promised to be the yacht race of the century, was scheduled for 24 September but there were to be a few more disappointments before that magic moment arrived.

Race Seven
24 September (abandoned)
Rerun 26 September
Australia II d. *Liberty* by 41 seconds

Alan Bond's intended 'rest' for the crew was well intentioned but it never materialized. After a morning on which *Australia II* was given a thorough check, Bertrand took her out to match wits in pre-start manoeuvres with Harold Cudmore, the Irish match-racing *aficionado* who had dropped out of the *Victory 83* syndicate following a disagreement with Peter de Savary.

There was to be no real rest for *Liberty*'s crew either. Most of them spent the day up at the Cove Haven Marina at Barrington, about 30 kilometres from Newport where *Liberty* was remeasured after 920 lb of lead were removed from her ballast package. Conner was determined to do whatever he could to stave off the Australian threat. Putting *Liberty* into her 'light-air mode' very nearly did the trick, allowing them to increase the size of her mainsail by about 22 square feet. Conner had used *Liberty*'s multiple-rating certificate to great advantage over the other defence candidates, challengers *Defender* and *Courageous*, during the trials. The others were not told that the NYYC's America's Cup Committee had given Conner special permission to use three different ratings, one for each 'mode' – light, medium and heavy air. In the end it was thought that all this chopping and changing might in some ways have acted against *Liberty*'s best interests.

On 24 September, after two abandoned attempts to start the seventh race, Conner announced that he would change *Liberty*'s ballast package again. Once more the crew had to endure the tedious six-hour ritual of towing to Barrington, hauling out and plumbing the boat dead vertical only then to be told at the last minute that the latest weather forecast meant they would be staying in their light-weather configuration after all. This was all perfectly legal but that did not stop Alan Bond labelling *Liberty* as a 'rule bender'. The conditions of the match put no limit on the number of times a yacht might be reballasted and remeasured during the series and that, specifically, was what Bond was objecting to.

'We came here to race one yacht, not three yachts,' he said, 'and this rule, if it can't be taken to the international jury and wiped out, is a disgrace.' Bondy was annoyed that Conner, having obtained three separate measurement certificates, had, in effect, three separate boats. 'At no stage in any yachting regatta in the world has a yacht been able to change [ballast],' he said. 'Next we'll have a different colour for each configuration because we won't know the yacht we're racing against.'

Bond said that his team was considering protesting to the Race Committee when the two yachts met on the starting line. 'It certainly is not the intent of the rule to change your yacht each day, and it never has been.' Ben, in contrast to Bond, saw nothing illegal or crooked in what the Americans were doing. 'It's all in the rule book,' he said. In Ben's view Bondy was just being Bondy, who he described as being like 'the sort of kid who sees a savage dog on the other side of a picket fence and, knowing that the dog can't get to him, he picks up a stick and clatters it down the fence just to drive the damn thing wild.'

There was another aborted start on Monday, 26 September when the 8–10-knot south-south-westerly wind shifted and officials called a halt at 12.08 p.m. after eight minutes of manoeuvring. Then, at 1.05 p.m. in a breeze of 205° the yacht race of the century finally got under way. It began with a great deal of caution. The boats circled warily and sometimes drove in and feinted. Those who had expected blood and guts at the end were disappointed. Dennis Conner knew only too well the extraordinary turning ability of the Australian boat.

Liberty appeared a lot more lively with so much lead taken out. With two minutes to the gun both boats approached the line on starboard, *Liberty* ready to go off to Conner's favourite right-hand side of the course and Bertrand happy to go to the left. *Liberty* tacked away and started on port. She crossed the line eight seconds ahead of *Australia II* and set out immediately, looking for the shifts that would hopefully help her compensate for *Australia II*'s phenomenal light-air ability. But it was *Australia II* that got them on the left and when they converged eighteen minutes after the gun she was a clear two lengths in front.

Two minutes later *Liberty* tacked on to starboard. *Australia II* crossed on port, three or four boat lengths ahead, and tacked on to starboard covering *Liberty*'s air. That forced Conner to take away on to port. When *Australia II* came about on port *Liberty* immediately tossed back to starboard. The Australians held on for four minutes which allowed Conner to split tacks and go a long way to the left. John Bertrand was severely criticized by the media for his failure to cover but as he explained later he did not have sufficient wind pressure to tack quickly and effectively cover *Liberty*. He was also convinced that the next shift would come from the right.

Instead it was a header from the left that knocked *Australia II* down toward *Liberty*'s line. The next time they crossed they were dead even. *Liberty* tacked on *Australia II*'s lee bow and forced Bertrand on to port to clear his air. The Australians had lost the advantage and the Americans now clamped a close cover on them. It was a tactical gain that at that stage seemed likely to keep the cup safely on its pedestal in the NYYC.

When *Liberty* came round the first mark twenty-nine seconds ahead there was wild cheering and a good deal of horn-blasting aboard the enormous spectator fleet. It was at this point that Alan Bond came down from the bridge and told Ben: 'Well, they can't win now. They're too stupid.' Ben thought he was right and remembers that, 'All I could think of was, what we are going to tell the smart-arse press afterwards? I thought they would crucify us.' Alan Bond, deeply upset and gloomy, returned to *Black Swan*'s bridge. Ben said: 'If Bond had to lose, he was going to take it on the jaw. He wasn't about to go below and blubber.'

The Americans picked up a further sixteen seconds to lead by forty-five seconds at the gybe mark. A 10° shift had converted the first broad reach into a very tight one but that also meant that the second reaching leg had become a square run, a point of sailing in which *Australia II* was clearly superior. They did what is known as a gybe-peel in swapping the star-cut spinnaker for a nicely rounded, mostly white bubble with green-and-gold bands about its middle. *Liberty* stuck with her first spinnaker and *Australia II* closed to within twenty-three seconds of *Liberty* at the bottom mark. *Black Knight* signalled the new course – 195°.

Conner sailed a magnificent second windward leg. At no stage did he allow Bertrand to escape from his cover. At the end of the second beat *Liberty*, giving by far the best light-air account of herself ever, had managed to stretch the gap to fifty-seven seconds. To many spectators it looked as if the boat race was all over. But *Australia II*'s incredible downwind speed over *Liberty* was to prove her trump card.

Soon after she rounded the mark *Liberty* gybed to port and sailed back towards the centre of the course to escape the so-called 'fence' effect of the spectator fleet, which not only blocked the breeze but threw up disturbed water as well. The Australians went precisely the opposite way after a beautiful bare-away spinnaker set. The Australians, instead of sailing into spectator slop, found themselves in fresh air.

Liberty, unlike most conventional 12-metre boats, is comparatively slow when she runs dead square. So Conner made five gybes, angling the breeze across his stern as much as possible to increase his boat's speed and use whatever shifts there were to his advantage. *Australia II*, which was almost as fast-running dead square as *Liberty* on a quartering run, simply assailed 'deeper', at smaller angles to the mark, and therefore had less distance to cover. Ben believes that *Australia II* gained so dramatically on *Liberty* on this leg because she had a better shape in the water. She had at least a $2\frac{1}{2}$-ton weight advantage over *Liberty* and, even more important, she had smaller, more efficient spinnakers which were better set and better trimmed than those aboard the American boat.

Two-thirds of the way to the bottom mark *Australia II* had run down *Liberty* and at the end of the leg she was twenty-one seconds ahead. It was an incredible moment watching that big white kite with its green-and-gold bars slide on past *Liberty*'s red, white and blue. Millions of bleary-eyed Australians, who had stayed

Australia II leads *Liberty* in Race Seven

up all night to watch the spectacle on television and listen on radio, sensed that victory was within reach. But there were still another agonizing 4.5 miles to go. And Dennis Conner was determined to fight every inch of the way.

Conner launched a desperate and sustained tacking duel. He tossed *Liberty* about forty-seven times and forty-seven times he was met by a grim Australian defence. John Bertrand had learned from bitter experience that he had to cover this man at all costs. *Liberty* tried the false tack twice, dummying to tack and then falling back to its original heading while *Australia II* was left hung-up head to wind and more committed to completing her tack. It went on for two minutes short of an hour. This was the supreme test of the crews' fitness. All the stamina and will power that had been built up over two, and in some cases, three years of effort was now being called upon. Neither crew was found wanting.

Conner realized that he was losing with every tack and in one last attempt to outfox the Australians, he lured them into the very edge of the spectator fleet on the starboard side of the layline, hoping that *Australia II* might become tangled up and trapped in the confused sea and air from the spectator vessels. Bertrand, however, remained calm and when he was certain that he could make the line, he turned and left Conner sailing away from the mark. All the Americans could do was turn and follow in his wake.

As *Australia II* approached the committee boat with victory within sight the Australians sat tense and silent, scared in the best tradition of superstitious sailors that any false move might somehow bring the mast tumbling down and allow Conner to sneak by. In those last moments one man did succumb to what must have been a dreadful desire to take a peek at the approaching line. John Longley

RACE 7

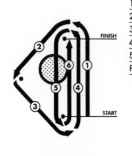

START	00:08	LIBERTY
1ST MARK	00:29	LIBERTY
2ND MARK	00:45	LIBERTY
3RD MARK	00:23	LIBERTY
4TH MARK	00:57	LIBERTY
5TH MARK	00:21	AUSTRALIA II
FINISH	00:41	AUSTRALIA II

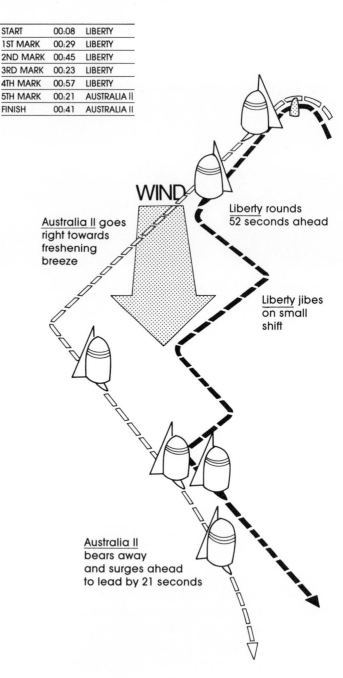

WIND

Australia II goes right towards freshening breeze

Liberty rounds 52 seconds ahead

Liberty jibes on small shift

Australia II bears away and surges ahead to lead by 21 seconds

RACE SEVEN
'*Australia II* was just faster downwind. The crew excelled itself in sailing the boat perfectly, and at times *Liberty* seemed to sail too deep and too slow, probably in desperation.' (Ben Lexcen)

The finish line at the final race

crept to the weatherside of *Australia II* so that he could peer round the head-sail. He sneaked back and whispered to winchman Brian Richardson: 'I think we're going to win the America's Cup.' He was immediately silenced by the other crew members and when they finally heard the boom of the cannon and the white smoke drifted past there was a strange, stunned quiet. John Bertrand covered his face with both hands. Colin Beashel remembers: 'No one spoke for a while. We all just sat there looking at each other, some of us grinning, some crying. I remember there were quite a few tears. I certainly let a few go. Hughie Treharne was the first to speak. "I don't believe it. We've actually won it." There was a bit of back-slapping and hand-shaking but then our thoughts turned to the boat. We knew we had to get the gear off her quickly because a great mob of spectators was heading our way. Somehow we just wanted to be together then, just the crew, Bondy, Warren and Ben. We were very close, like brothers. I think that closeness is one of the things I'll remember most about that cup campaign.'

For Ben with the end came a feeling of tremendous relief. All through the last leg of the climactic race he had suffered acute anxiety. But now it was over and for the first time in twelve long years of nothing but 12-metres he could relax. He claims it was all a bit of an anti-climax. 'It was extraordinary when we got back to the dock. There were thousands of people yelling and screaming and spraying champagne everywhere. I thought it was a little bit pointless. After all, it was only a silly bloody boat race.'

When the Australians came back into Newport's historic harbour there were tens of thousands of people waiting to give them a hero's welcome. They clambered up on roofs, boats, cars and anything that could give them even a glimpse of the team that had, after 132 years, ended the NYYC's domination of the America's Cup – the most precious trophy in world yachting. The dock was crowded with rubber runabouts, kyaks, canoes, dinghies, luxury gin-palaces and people swimming fully clothed. Helicopters hovered overhead. People went mad in the fearful din of exploding firecrackers, cannons, sirens, horns and screaming. Scores of police came in to push the crowds back when they started a stampede that threatened to tear down the *Australia II* dockyard fence.

A great chant started: 'Let's see the keel, let's see the keel, let's see the keel.' Eventually Alan Bond jumped up on to *Black Swan*'s stern and, like a histrionic conductor, raised his arm to give the signal to hoist away. 'Show them,' Bondy yelled, 'let's show the world.' At long last the weird and wonderful secret keel would be revealed. As it rose out of the murky depths of Newport Harbour it looked almost alive, like some strange underwater creature.

First the thick, rounded, reverse-raked leading edge came out of the water all white with a blue camouflage stripe. Then the wings – great thick, strange-looking wings that swept down and aft like the graceful Delta wings of a Vulcan Bomber. When they saw the keel, some people cried. They leapt into the water to hug, kiss,

Ben, with John Bertrand and Alan Bond in the background

Australia II's keel

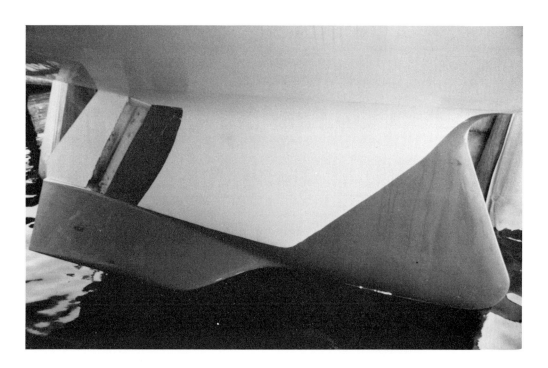

caress and pour champagne over the docile-looking secret weapon. Finally they sat on it.

Alan Bond stood back and watched with an enormous grin on his face. It was a wonderful, once in a lifetime moment. Later he took every one of his crew men into a press conference crammed with 600 journalists and media people from all over the world. There the crew were introduced one by one as if they were all stars at an Academy Award gala. And indeed they were. That night the cup was brought to Newport in an armoured van. Some of the more conservative members of the NYYC had, according to Alan Bond, tried to hold a small, formal handing over ceremony in New York which would involve only the syndicate heads and the senior club officers. Bond wanted the ceremony held in Newport so that all the Australian crew could take part. After consultations with the Newport Preservation Society, the NYYC agreed that the ceremony should take place on the terrace of Newport's grandest house, the great William K. Vanderbilt's mansion, Marble House.

On Tuesday, 27 September, nearly 1,000 people assembled for the ceremony.

Inconspicuous among all the assembled guests was Normie Wright – the 'King of the Brisbane River' – who had first encouraged the young Bob Miller to take up designing. The NYYC's distinguished and eloquent Commodore, Robert Stone, produced the cup that had remained hidden away in the private recesses of the New York Club since the turn of the century. He also produced the 4-foot steel bolt that had fastened the cup to its oaken plinth for so many years. The bolt was originally installed after cleaners accidentally knocked the cup off its pedestal and bent the ornate neck. Tiffany's, the famous New York jewellers, fixed it but ever since it has had a slight lean to one side and required the bolt to anchor it securely. Commodore Stone displayed a nice sense of humour when he presented Ben with a squashed hub cap in lieu of the 'America's Cup plate', which he had once threatened to create by steamrolling the 'auld mug'.

Back in Australia the entire country seemed to have come to a standstill. The morning traffic jam that usually chokes the Sydney Harbour Bridge was almost an hour late as tens of thousands of people stayed at home to watch the final moments of the race and listen to the commentary on the radio. At the Royal Perth Yacht Club Prime Minister Bob Hawke was drenched in champagne as he joined the celebrations. In cities and towns right across Australia complete strangers greeted and hugged each other in a manner unprecedented since the end of the Second World War. The winged victory brought Australians together, giving them a common focus, a talking point. The celebrations went on for a very long time. In October the Western Australian Premier declared a state-wide holiday, *Australia II* day. Over 400,000 people are reported to have turned out from Fremantle to Perth to welcome the crew home. There were civic receptions, keys to the city and medallions bestowed, speeches and handshakes. All of Australia, it seemed, wanted to say, 'Well done, *Australia II*.'

Ben and Warren Jones with the America's Cup

Chapter Seven

After the Cup

At a stroke *Australia II*'s winged victory had rendered redundant $50 million worth of 12-metre yachts around the world. But there was still uncertainty about the keel's future and this had worried Ben throughout the America's Cup even in the moment of victory. He was expecting to have to face another fight when the fourteen members of the IYRU's Keelboat Committee met two months later in November 1983 to give their official verdict on the keel. There were still powerful men within the New York Yacht Club who, Ben believed, wanted to discredit him. He felt that the meeting would be 'a sort of last-ditch stand for the forces of reaction'.

When on 14 November the IYRU committee voted 'without dissent' to approve winged keels for 12-metre yachts, Ben was astonished. *Australia II*'s keel was 5 feet 2 inches (1.57 metres) wide, and the committee agreed to allow future wings to be as wide as 11 feet $9\frac{3}{4}$ inches (3.6 metres), equal to the minimum beam of a 12-metre. Ben assigned all royalty payments on the patent of the winged keel to the IYRU.

The Offshore Racing Council, however, responded very differently. For over a decade ocean-racing owners had been suffering at the hands of designers constantly contriving to exploit loopholes in the rating rules. As designers succeeded in making names for themselves each season their work invariably rendered champion boats obsolete. The owners of ocean racers, who ultimately control the sport through the officials they elect, made it clear that they wanted as few changes as possible in their style of boats. They felt that, at last, they had established a set of workable measurement rules and a rating system that gave most well-sailed

Homecoming, Sydney Airport, 1983. Ben and friend, Kev Koala

yachts a reasonable chance. Not surprisingly the rule-makers for all ocean-racing yachts decided by seventeen votes to three against the winged keel.

Ben was privately delighted by the ban. 'If it had gone the other way the Americans would have caught up with us very quickly. They have a vast turnover of boats in the States and I'm sure that all that practical trial and error would have produced some super-advanced variations. Now they have to learn in the tank like everyone else and that will be both expensive and difficult.' Despite claims that American designers have already pushed the winged keel concept to extraordinary new performance levels, Ben is quietly confident: 'I still think we will have an edge when it comes to winged keels. It will be a fine edge though. We won't be ahead by much.' One American designer wrote to tell Ben that he had a winged keel that made *Australia II*'s look 'crude': 'I don't believe that. I think the Americans are kidding themselves. They have probably made a big, swept-back, space-age, comic-book thing that just looks fast. We will have to wait and see what happens on the race course.' While the Americans are investing millions to perfect the winged keel, the city of Perth is preparing itself for what promises to be the world's biggest 12-metre regatta – the 1986/7 America's Cup Challenge – which will be sailed just north of Fremantle Harbour.

Immediately after the Australian win the Royal Perth Yacht Club was inundated with enquiries from would-be challengers. By 30 April 1984, the challenge deadline, twenty-three challengers had come forward with the required entry fee, which the Royal Perth had increased from the $3,000 demanded by the New York Yacht Club to $A12,000. There were nine American challengers, four from Italy, three from France, two from Canada and one each from Britain, Switzerland, Germany and New Zealand. By contrast, Royal Perth was able to put forward the names of only three definite defence syndicates.

The staggering number of challengers will make the 1986/7 Cup series three times bigger than the 1983 races and one of the world's biggest regattas. The Western Australian state government has announced plans to spend more than $A4 million on a vast new marina to cope with not only the racing yachts but also their support crafts.

The American Yacht Clubs include the New York Yacht Club's *America II* syndicate, which plans to spend $12 million on as many as three new boats. Their helmsman is to be John Kolius. The San Diego Yacht Club has also budgeted $12 million. It will have Dennis Conner as its helmsman. The Chicago Yacht Club has engaged world Star-class champion skipper Buddy Melges as its helmsman. Other American challenges have come from Yale University's Yale Corinthian Yacht Club in New Haven, Connecticut; the Blue Dolphin Yacht Club from Newport Beach, California; the St Francis Yacht Club from San Francisco; the Sag Harbour Yacht Club, New York, and the St Petersburg Yacht Club from St Petersburg, Florida.

The four Italian challengers include the Aga Khan's Yacht Club, Costa Smeralda; the Yacht Club Italiano; the Yacht Club, Porto Fino; and the Yacht Club Nautico Marina di Carrara. The three from France are Société Nautique de Marseilles; Société des Régates Rochelaise and the Yacht Club de France. The Canadians are the Royal Nova Scotia Yacht Squadron and the Secret Cove Yacht Club, which campaigned in 1983 with *Canada I.* The Royal Thames Yacht Club is the sole British contender.

The Swiss Club Société Nautique de Genève holds its annual regatta at Cannes, on the French Riviera, and therefore overcomes any objections which may have been levelled through the Deed of Gift's exclusionary clause relating to challenging clubs being on an arm of the sea. The German entry comes from Potsdamer Yacht Club in West Berlin. West Berlin is connected to the North Sea at Hamburg by the Havel and Elbe river systems, but whether that constitutes a legitimate arm of the sea remains to be seen.

Finally, from across the Tasman sea comes the Royal New Zealand Yacht Squadron with its first ever America's Cup challenge. The last entry came from Tokyo Ocean Yacht Club.

The Western Australian state government and the Royal Perth Yacht Club have set up a committee to decide how to organize the cup challenge. Shortly after the 1983 victory the committee examined ideas for possible rule changes and agreed on two which they believe will promote better racing in 1987.

The 1986/7 series will have a new course. It will be exactly the same length, 24.1 nautical miles, but will have two extra legs, a beat and a square run. From the start there will be a $3\frac{1}{4}$-mile beat, then a square run, a second beat, a starboard spinnaker reach out to a wing mark, a port reach to the leeward mark, a third beat, a second square run and a final beat home.

The changes are necessary, in Ben's view, because the old-style course with its 4.5-mile beats could not safely be fitted in between Rottnest Island and the Fremantle shore. 'With this set-up we will have the racing yachts coming in very close to the shore so that people who can't get out on a boat will still be able to see at least part of the race. We think they will come around the bottom mark no more than 400 yards from the beach. It will be more of a spectacle with more mark roundings and more legs. It will be more difficult to pass because we won't have the long legs, but in another sense it will be easier for foul-ups to occur at the mark roundings. It would have been pretty boring if we had stuck to the old long legs. The wind off Fremantle is so steady that the boat in front would be covering perfectly all the way.'

The enormous costs associated with running a regatta of this size, together with the provision of facilities for the racing yachts, their crews and backers, has posed a huge problem for the authorities. Ben is very critical of the open-hearted approach of the Western Australian organizers who are eager to extend a genuine

welcome to the visitors while capitalizing on the international attention which
will focus on Perth and Fremantle. 'Poor little Perth is the world's most isolated
capital city,' Ben said, 'and they are behaving like country boys trying to show
how sophisticated they are by helping the foreigners get established. If the Perth
city fathers have their way they'll turn the America's Cup into a sort of Olympic
Games where the host country provides accommodation and dock facilities and all
mod-cons. They're actually helping to beat the Australian defence. That's not what
the NYYC did for 132 years. I'm sure that providing for all the foreign competitors
will do wonders for Perth's image and Australia's international reputation but it's
not the way we are going to keep the cup for 132 years. That's the way to give it
away, first pop.'

The state government, undaunted by Ben's pessimistic words, plans to finance
a new $3 million marina complex at Fremantle, which will house up to twenty
12-metre yachts. Special concrete aprons, finger berths and hydraulic haul-out
facilities are to be put in at government expense and leased back to the various
competing syndicates. The *America II* syndicate arrived in Fremantle in March
1984 and announced plans to spend up to $12 million on their campaign to
regain the cup. The campaign is scheduled to begin in October 1984 with the
arrival of an NYYC trial horse and a training squad of fifteen. The Italians will
arrive in November from Sardinia.

Five months after the cup a South Australian syndicate announced plans to
build a cup defender to Ben's design. The lines of this boat were being as closely
guarded as those of *Australia II*. Ben claims that the boat, which will be called
Jubilee and will be a promotional tool for South Australia's 150th birthday celebrations, will have a more efficient winged keel than *Australia II*.

A third cup defence contender is to be designed by a young and largely unknown
Perth naval architect, John Swarbrick, in conjunction with five-times world 18-
footer champion Iain Murray, the youthful skipper of Sydney's ill-fated 1983 cup
contender, *Advance*.

This syndicate will be financed almost exclusively by Western Australian multi-
millionaire businessman Kevin Parry, who is prepared to spend up to $A6 million
on two new boats. Ironically Alan Bond now finds himself in a strange situation:
he is, in essence, contracted to assist in his own downfall. Under the terms of his
package agreement with the South Australian syndicate he has to supply not only
Ben's design expertise but also state-of-the-art technology in rig and sails and
details of the brilliant management plans which played such a vital role in
Australia's victory. This means that it is possible that he will not be running the
show in 1986/7, a role that he could have secured for himself by simply refusing
to help the other defenders. But that would have almost certainly guaranteed the
loss of the cup.

Australia III will have to race against at least two new boats and Bond will be

How it all began – five boys and a model boat. Not quite the map pool at Newcastle: Ben Lexcen, Warren Jones, Sir James Hardy and Bruno Troublé at the Tuileries Gardens Model Pond, Paris, 1984

playing a very careful waiting game, delaying construction of his own boat until the performance of the new boats can be assessed. It is possible that he may keep open an option which would allow him to build a second new boat as late as July 1986.

When Ben is asked what his new boats will look like, he gives only the broadest outline: 'I would imagine there would be slightly less sail area and that the boats would have a longer waterline length. There will be stronger winds in Perth. It's not going to be such a tricky place to sail. It's just going to be a speed-boat race, so acceleration won't be so important. That means the boat can be a little heavier. We will have to go for all-out speed. The breeze should be about 18 knots. You can't sacrifice everything and go for a heavy-weather boat because you could get light-weather races in the trials which might be enough to eliminate you if they were critical big-points races. I imagine the boats designed for Perth conditions will have 20-foot booms instead of 30-foot ones and they would perhaps weigh a couple of thousand pounds more and be a foot or two longer. Why longer? The longer boat has a higher potential top speed. A heavier boat is stiffer, so that also helps speed on the wind. The sail area is just a straight-out horsepower number, so the bigger the sails the more horsepower you've got.'

In 1987 Ben will be fifty, 'the big Five-O', he says with a half-wistful, half-impish, look. He wonders what it is that motivates apparently sane people to spend millions of pounds and years of their lives competing for the America's Cup. 'I'm already asking myself why I'm checking into this madhouse yet again. It's like hitting myself on the head with a bloody great hammer. All I get is headaches. When you analyse this whole 12-metre thing you have to wonder why people subject themselves to all those hassles. There has to be an element of madness in there. But then if you look at the mega-millionaires involved, there aren't many things in the world that can pander to their egos as much as the America's Cup summer does. They're on the world stage for three months. And let's face it, they love all that media attention. Even the richest guys can't get that sort of attention unless they cause a bloody war. Nothing else allows them to command so much world attention so easily and so cheaply. And if they succeed it's incredible. Those mega-dollar guys run on hyperpower. That's what the America's Cup comes down to in the end, a huge ego trip. Why else would you do it? We all want to be world famous. That's something that has always driven me. I achieved a degree of notoriety over the America's Cup win but now my ego is saying I've got to go on and defend the damned thing. It's no longer enough to have won it. I used to think I'd be somehow set free if I won the cup but it's not true at all. I'm still a prisoner of the auld mug. Now the big thing is to defend it, to hang on to it, to show the Yanks that it wasn't just a fluke.'

Index

Page numbers in *italic* refer to illustrations